South Island

10	**Ferry to the South Island**	p68
11	**Dunedin and the Otago Peninsula**	p71
12	**Akaroa**	p76
13	**Hanmer Springs**	p80
14	**Christchurch to Queenstown**	p83
15	**Arthur's Pass and West Coast**	p86
16	**Queenstown**	p92
17	**Arrowtown**	p95
18	**Milford Sound**	p98

INSIGHT GUIDES

NEW ZEALAND
Step by Step

APA PUBLICATIONS L

Part of the Langenscheidt Publishing Group

CONTENTS

Introduction
About This Book   4
Recommended Tours   6

Overview
Country Overview   10
Food and Drink   14
Shopping   18
Entertainment   20
History: Key Dates   22

Walks and Tours
The North Island
1. Auckland   26
2. Around Auckland   33
3. Northland   36

4. Coromandel
    Peninsula   42
5. Tauranga District   46
6. Rotorua   49
7. Taupo   54
8. Wellington   60
9. The Wairarapa   65

The South Island
10. Ferry to the
    South Island   68
11. Dunedin and the
    Otago Peninsula   71
12. Akaroa   76
13. Hanmer Springs   80

14. Christchurch to
    Queenstown   83
15. Arthur's Pass and
    the West Coast   86
16. Queenstown   92
17. Arrowtown   95
18. Milford Sound   98

Directory
A–Z   102
Accommodation   112
Restaurants   120

Credits and Index
Picture Credits   124
Index   126

ABOUT THIS BOOK

This *Step by Step Guide* has been produced by the editors of Insight Guides, whose books have set the standard for visual travel guides since 1970. With top-quality photography and authoritative recommendations, this guidebook brings you the very best of New Zealand in a series of 18 tailor-made tours.

WALKS AND TOURS

The tours in the book provide something to suit all budgets, tastes and trip lengths, so whether you are an architecture buff, a lover of flora and fauna or have kids to entertain, you will find an option to suit. From the subtropical north to the temperate south, all the wonders of the country are presented, with the tours grouped around five geographical hubs: Auckland, Rotorua and Wellington in the North Island and Christchurch and Queenstown in the South Island. There are walking tours of the main city sights as well as day- and multi-day tours of the surrounding areas.

We recommend that you read the whole of a tour before setting out. This should help you to familiarise yourself with the route and enable you to plan

where to stop for refreshments – options for this are shown in the 'Food and Drink' boxes, recognisable by the knife and fork sign, on most pages.

For our pick of the walks by theme, consult 'Recommended Tours For...' *(see pp.6–7)*.

OVERVIEW

The tours are set in context by this introductory section, which gives an overview of the country to set the scene, plus background information on food and drink, shopping and entertainment. A succinct history timeline highlights the key events that have shaped New Zealand over the centuries.

DIRECTORY

Also supporting the tours is a Directory chapter, comprising a user-friendly, clearly organised A–Z of practical information, our pick of where to stay while you are in the country, and select restaurant listings; these eateries complement the more low-key cafés and restaurants that feature within the tours themselves and are intended to offer a wider choice for evening dining.

Above: New Zealand highlights.

The Authors

Many of the tours in this guide were originally conceived by **Craig Dowling**, who has lived and worked as a journalist in New Zealand's three largest cities, Auckland, Wellington and Christchurch, gaining a broad insight into the diversity that makes it such an incredible country. The tours have been thoroughly revised and updated for this *Step by Step Guide* by **Donna Blaber**, a travel journalist based in Waipu. Donna has also added a new introductory chapter, a new entertainment chapter and new listings for the Directory at the back of the book.

FOOD AND DRINK

Kiwi cooking is distinguished by ingredients that are fresh and flavourful, and a visit that fuses a medley of influences, reflecting the country's cultural diversity. A latecomer to the world of wine-making, it now also produces outstanding vintages that are red and acclaimed worldwide.

Fresh and vibrant, New Zealand cuisine is often described as Pacific Rim, as it draws much of its inspiration from Europe, Asia and Polynesia. This blend of influences has created a mouthwatering range of flavours and food that can be sampled in cafés, restaurants and lodges nationwide. Innovative chefs make clever use of tasty ingredients freshly harvested from the garden, land and sea – which, in the company of award-winning local wines, make for New Zealand gastronomic experience among the best in the world.

While food and beverage production has long been the linchpin of New Zealand's prosperity and a leading export earner, it's the boom of unique, quality produce and ethnic influences that has allowed a national food identity to evolve. Nowadays New Zealand's worldwide reputation for award-winning produce draws tourists from afar to the source, and food tourism is developing at a rapid rate.

TRADITIONAL DINING

The country's cuisine culture is also distinctive in the way that New Zealanders prefer to eat an environment that is as relaxed and unaffected as possible, in tune with the laid-back Kiwi psyche.

Summer usually means endless barbecues and alfresco dining, with the emphasis on fresh, simple fare. Barbecues have long been a big part of the Kiwi culture, and Pacific influences, organic or home-grown produce, and indigenous foods make it unique. Fare such as lamb, venison, fresh fish including crayfish (lobster) and other shellfish such as pipi, tuatua and scallops, are fresh-harvested and plentiful.

The Hangi

For an authentic New Zealand eating experience, try a traditional Maori hangi (pronounced 'hung-ee'), cooked underground. A deep hole is dug, then lined with red hot stones and covered with vegetation. The food (chicken, pork, lamb, potatoes, kumara – sweet potato – and other vegetables) is placed on top, then the whole town is spread with water and sealed, and left to steam for several hours, giving a smoky taste. Traditionally, all members of a whanau (family) come for the feast, with stereotypical gender roles the norm: the men digging and working on the hole, and the women preparing the food to go in it. Several tourist locations, including Rotorua in the North Island, invite visitors to join in and experience hangi culture. (see p.13)

SEAFOOD

Fish is abundant and of very good quality in New Zealand, with varieties including freshwater salmon, sole and flounder. If you want to eat trout, however, note that you will have to catch your own, as it is illegal to sell it (see p.17). A seasonal delicacy is tuatua (whitebait), a tiny seasnow-like fish, that can be enjoyed nationwide, although it has become synonymous with the South Island's West Coast.

On your travels, look out for roadside stalls selling succulent crayfish and/or freshly smoked mussels or fish. The sublime flavour of crayfish can also be enjoyed at any good seafood restaurant; try Whitet Morph (Kaikoura, South Island) or Harbourside Seafood Bar & Grill (Quay Street, Auckland).

Throughout the year, shellfish such as mussels, pipi and tuatua can be gathered freely from the beach. Greenlipped mussels, paua (abalone) and oysters – the Pacific oyster, the rock oyster and the famed Bluff oyster – can also be found on menus nationwide.

British visitors may be pleased to learn that fish and chips are a popular takeaway meal in New Zealand, served in the traditional way: piping hot and wrapped in paper.

NATIONAL SPECIALITIES

Your New Zealand culinary experience is incomplete until you savour the sweet, creamy stickiness of pavlova, the national dessert. In addition, it's worth looking out for some food products that offer an entirely new taste sensation. These include hokey pokey ice cream (vanilla ice cream with toffee bits in it,

Margin Tips
Shopping tips, historical facts, handy hints and information on activities help visitors to make the most of their time in New Zealand.

Key Facts Box
This box gives details of the distance covered on the tour, plus an estimate of how long it should take. It also states where the route starts and finishes, and gives key travel information, such as which days are best to do the route, or handy transport tips.

Footers
Look here for the tour name, a map reference and the main attraction on the double page.

Food and Drink
Recommendations of where to stop for refreshment are given in these boxes. The numbers prior to each restaurant/café name link to references in the main text. Restaurants in the Food and Drink boxes are plotted on the individual tour maps.

The $ signs at the end of each entry reflect the approximate cost of a two-course meal for one, with one glass of house wine. These should be seen as a guide only. Price ranges, also quoted on the inside back flap for easy reference, are as follows:

$$$$	NZ$80 and above
$$$	NZ$60–80
$$	NZ$40–60
$	NZ$40 and below

Route Map
Detailed cartography shows the tour clearly plotted with numbered dots. For more detailed mapping, see the pull-out map slotted inside the back cover.

ANIMAL-LOVERS

Enjoy whale-watching off the coast at Kaikoura (tour 10), visit Akaroa to spot dolphins, fur seals and sea birds (tour 12) and spend a couple of hours at Kelly Tarlton's aquarium for the lowdown on sea life in New Zealand (tour 2).

RECOMMENDED TOURS FOR...

ART-LOVERS

The country's top galleries include the Auckland Art Gallery (tour 1), which houses a fantastic collection of works by Kiwi and Pacific island artists.

CHILDREN

Visit Kelly Tarlton's aquarium (tour 2), discover Kiwi wildlife at Rainbow Springs in Rotorua (tour 6) and look out for seals in the Wairarapa region (tour 9).

DAREDEVILS

Try rafting waterfalls around Rotorua (tour 5), glacier hiking and ice-climbing on the Franz Josef and Fox glaciers (tour 15) or bungy-jumping where the craze originated, near Queenstown (tours 16 and 17), the self-styled 'Adventure Capital of the World'.

FOOD AND WINE

Enjoy a vineyard tour at Martinborough, the heart of the Marlborough wine industry (tour 9), in the Waipara Valley wine region (tour 13) or in the Gibbston Valley (tour 17), near Queenstown.

GEOTHERMAL ACTIVITY

For spouting geysers, bubbling mud pools and natural hot springs, visit Rotorua (tour 6) or Taupo (tour 7).

HISTORY HUNTERS

Retrace the past at Auckland's War Memorial Museum (tour 1), at Waitangi in Northland, the birthplace of the nation and home to the country's founding document, the Treaty of Waitangi (tour 3), and at the Museum of New Zealand in Wellington (tour 8).

PAMPERING

Take time out in your own freshly dug warm pool on Hot Water Beach (tour 4), at Rotorua's Polynesian Spa (tour 6), in a hot saltwater pool near Mount Maunganui (tour 5) and at Hanmer Springs Thermal Resort and Spa (tour 13).

SPORTY TYPES

Try yachting or watch the All Blacks in Auckland (tour 1), join in the 'Round the Bays' run (tour 2), hike up Flagstaff Hill in the Bay of Islands (tour 3) or surf near Whangamata (tour 4).

UNBEATABLE VIEWS

There are so many unbeatable views in New Zealand that it's hard to summarise, but highlights include the views around Aoraki/Mount Cook, the country's highest mountain (tour 14), the scenery around the Franz Josef and Fox glaciers (tour 15) and around Milford Sound (tour 18).

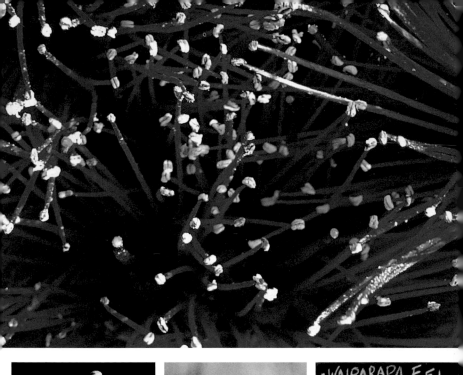

- WAIRARAPA EEL
- KAPITI CHEESE
- COROMANDEL SMOKED SEAFOOD
- BLACK PUDDING

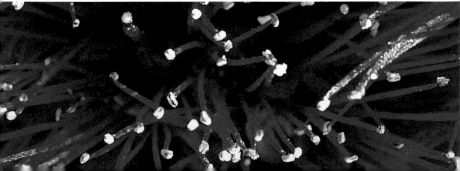

OVERVIEW

An overview of New Zealand's geography, customs and culture, plus illuminating background information on food and drink, shopping, entertainment and history.

COUNTRY OVERVIEW   10

FOOD AND DRINK   14

SHOPPING   18

ENTERTAINMENT   20

HISTORY: KEY DATES   22

COUNTRY OVERVIEW

New Zealand's archipelago of around 700 islands offers a wealth of dramatic scenery, from the exquisite beauty of the Southern Alps and Milford Sound, to the bush-wrapped solitude of Lake Waikaremoana and the boiling surprises of the thermal regions.

Local Birdlife
New Zealand's unique birds include the flightless kiwi *(above, top)*, the unofficial national symbol, from which its inhabitants take their nickname. It has hairlike feathers and a long, slender bill. Kiwi birds are only active at night in wilderness areas. The country's cheekiest feathered friend is the kea *(above, bottom)*, an alpine parrot, renowned for its fearlessness of humans. Other flightless birds include the weka and the endangered kakapo, the world's largest parrot.

New Zealand is situated in the South Pacific between latitudes 34° and 37° South. It is a long, narrow country, lying roughly north–south and comprising two main islands – the North and the South – separated by the Cook Strait. It is surrounded by the Pacific Ocean on its east coast and the Tasman Sea on its west coast. At 269,057 sq km (103,883 sq miles), it is slightly larger than the British Isles. Two-thirds of the country is mountainous and dissected by swift-flowing rivers, deep alpine lakes and subtropical forest. Its highest mountain is Aoraki Mount Cook, located in the Southern Alps.

Meteoric Rise to Fame

New Zealand's remoteness from the rest of the world has served both to limit the number of visitors and to preserve the land from over-exploitation. Those who did come were delighted by what they found packed into a comparatively small country. But what was known to only a number of enthusiasts became known to millions in 2001, with the release of the movie *The Lord of the Rings: The Fellowship of the Ring*, directed by native son Peter Jackson. Cast in the role of Middle Earth, New Zealand's spectacular landscapes became travel's worst-kept secret.

GETTING AROUND

For the independent traveller, New Zealand's geography, while providing scenes of unsurpassed beauty, poses some difficulties in terms of time. The country's length and rough-hewn nature, plus the division into two main islands, makes travelling time often longer than you expect. The bottom line is that when your vacation time is limited, it is impossible to see everything the country has to offer.

Most of the tours in this book focus on five main hubs – Auckland, Rotorua, Wellington, Christchurch and Queenstown – with a number of additional tours guiding you around the attractions in the rest of the country (the historic Bay of Islands; the beautiful beaches of Coromandel Peninsula; the adventure activities of Lake Taupo; the wineries of Wairarapa; the stunning glaciers of the South Island's West Coast, and the majesty of Milford Sound). If time allows, the tours can be linked together for an extensive north–south, or south–north, exploration of the whole country.

Travel Tips

If time is at a premium, it may help to use domestic flights to travel between

the main city hubs, then hire a car to access regional attractions. With its quiet, well-maintained roads, New Zealand is the perfect destination to tour by car. New Zealanders take seriously their commitment to protecting, as well as making accessible, the beauty of their natural environment.

NORTH ISLAND

Auckland and Northland

In subtropical Northland, proud forests of majestic kauri trees, some thousands of years old, share space with its gum-digging past. Gnarled red-blossoming pohutukawa trees (known as New Zealand Christmas trees) cling to windswept cliffs over golden beaches, and green rolling hills of farmland span from coast to coast. Thermal activity abounds: there's Auckland, built on extinct volcanoes; Rotorua, famous for its intense thermal activity in the form of geysers, hot springs and pools of boiling mud; and one of New Zealand's most special experiences: digging your own warm spa in the sand at Coromandel's Hot Water Beach *(see p.45)*.

Lake Taupo and Wellington

At the heart of the North Island lies Lake Taupo *(see p.57)*, New Zealand's largest lake: a huge volcanic crater fed by the mountains of the Central Plateau. Hidden beneath hills beside a crater-formed harbour, the capital city of Wellington is the departure point to the magnificent South Island, home to only one quarter of the country's population.

SOUTH ISLAND

The South Island provides travellers with an awe-inspiring panorama of majestic snowy mountains, dripping rainforest, silent fiords and sounds, ancient glaciers, wide-open plains and sparkling blue lakes and rivers. This is a place of grandeur and solitude, where visitors really can become at one with nature, in the shadow of the Southern Alps. These mountains, a spine of jagged peaks running the length of the South Island, were formed by a collision of tectonic plates, which, in a bid to outdo each other, force the mountains upwards by some 10mm (⅓in) per year.

As it is, the Southern Alps rise to heights of over 3,000m (9,843ft) in places, with Aoraki Mount Cook, New Zealand's highest mountain, dominating the range at 3,750m (12,303ft).

Above from far left: pohutukawa tree; Rere Falls, near Gisborne, in the East Cape (North Island); extreme mountain biking in the Southern Alps (South Island); wine country in the Canterbury region of the South Island.

Green Philosophy
The Maori story of creation explains that land and human beings are all one – flesh and clay from the same source material. The indigenous Maori emotional attachment to place is profound and has influenced *Pakeha* (European) culture, contributing to the national belief that 'clean and green' is a philosophy, not just a tourism marketing tool.

Left: footprints on the beach.

The West Coast

The West Coast offers a wealth of contrasting scenery, from dense forests of beech, to deep fiords and the icy tongues of Franz Josef and Fox glaciers *(see pp. 90–1)*, while the picturesque lakeside townships of Wanaka, Queenstown and Te Anau provide a base for adventure in the great outdoors.

To the east, the city of Christchurch itself is largely out of bounds due to the devastating earthquake that struck in early 2011. It is hoped that rebuilding efforts will make this attractive city visitor-ready again in the near future.

CLIMATE AND SEASONS

New Zealand's climate ranges from subtropical in the Northland to temperate/cool in the deep south. Places such as Invercargill on the southern coast of the South Island can be bitterly cold in winter, when southerly winds blow up from Antarctica. In terms of seasons, summer runs from December to February, autumn from March to May, winter from June to August, and spring from September to November.

Clothing

Whatever the season, it's essential to bring umbrellas and waterproofs, as a typical day in Auckland alternates between showers and sun. In the South Island, Fiordland and the West Coast have very high rainfall – Milford Sound gets over 6m (20ft) of rain a year.

Alpine weather is notoriously changeable, so those planning on visiting mountainous regions should bring plenty of warm clothing, even in summer. Take broken-in walking boots if you're planning on doing any hiking.

Dress is tidy but casual, although some pubs and hotel bars frown on jeans, jandals (flip-flops) and bare feet.

ACTIVITIES

Given New Zealand's diverse, remarkable terrain, it's not surprising that outdoor activities are huge business here. The following is a brief description of the main ones; for more information, visit the Tourism New Zealand website: www.newzealand.com.

Bungy-Jumping and Skydiving

New Zealand is where the craze for bungy-jumping began, and you can still throw yourself off a ledge with a rubber band attached to your ankles at many (often spectacular) places across the country. If jumping from a ledge with a rubber band tied to your legs is too passé for you, how about a tandem skydive? The bonus with this thrill is the stunning view offered by the plane ride as you circle up above the drop zone.

Fishing, Dolphins and Whales

New Zealand's waters are a breeding ground for a variety of native and introduced fish species, notably trout and salmon, as well as big game, and the country is well regarded for the angling opportunities it presents. Whether you hire a guide or head out on your own, you're assured of a good catch.

Alternatively, you can get up close and personal with dolphins at several

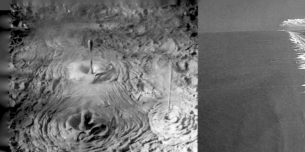

locations around the country, by hopping aboard a boat tour. Whale-watching tours are available in Kaikoura *(see p.70)*.

Jet-Boating and Rafting

Swift-flowing and broad, shallow rivers meant that traditional boats were next to useless in many of New Zealand's waterways. A new type of vessel – the jet-boat – was consequently developed here. Visitors can hop aboard for thrilling high-speed rides at several locations nationwide.

Another great way to experience New Zealand's fast-flowing rivers is in a raft. Rivers range from grade 1 (easy) to grade 5 (extreme), and trips vary from a few hours to a few days.

Snowsports

The rugged terrain offers a wide range of skiing in winter, typically at much lower prices than in Europe or the US. North Island commercial ski fields include Whakapapa and Turoa, both on the slopes of Mount Ruapehu, while in the South Island Queenstown offers a range of fields within easy reach, as does the city of Christchurch.

LANGUAGE

New Zealand has two official languages, English and Maori. Nearly everyone speaks English (with a distinctive, often nasal, accent). New Zealand has adopted standard English grammar and spelling, but has also added some 'Kiwi-isms' to the vocabulary. You may hear, for instance, the word 'grotty', meaning dirty, 'chilly bin', a portable cooler used for picnics, or 'grog', for alcohol.

Maori

Maori is a language undergoing a renaissance. It is taught in schools and is commonly spoken as a first language in several parts of the North Island. Maori influence is strong throughout the country in place names, and many words have entered common usage, for example: *Pakeha*, meaning a person of European descent; *kia ora*, for hello; *kai*, for food; *koha*, if a donation is required; and *hangi*, a style of Maori cooking.

Pronunciation is not difficult, once you master the vowels, which often occur alongside each other but are pronounced separately: a as in 'car'; e as in 'men'; i like 'ea' in 'bean'; o like 'aw' in 'paw'; u like 'oo' in 'moon'. The only complex sounds are wh, pronounced more or less like 'f', and ng, pronounced like the 'ng' in 'singing'. Syllables are given equal stress. Maori words do not take an 's' to form the plural.

The Ultimate Linguistic Test

If you feel that you've gained a certain proficiency in the Maori language, try one of the longest place names in the world, attached to a hill in the Hawke's Bay area. In its shortened version it's called Taumatawhakatangihangako-auauotamateapokaiwhenuakitanatahu. It means, 'Where Tamatea of the big knees, the man who slid down, climbed and consumed mountains and is known as the land-eater, played the flute to his beloved'.

Geology

New Zealand's separation from other land masses about 100 million years ago allowed many ancient plants and animals to survive and evolve in isolation. For this reason its landscape features an unrivalled variety of landforms, as well as unique flora and fauna.
In a couple of days' driving it is possible to see everything from mountain ranges and sandy beaches to lush rainforests, active volcanoes, glaciers, sounds and fiords.

Government

New Zealand is a sovereign, independent democratic state and a member of both the United Nations and the Commonwealth. The government is elected every three years under the proportional representation system called MMP. The Government's leader is the Prime Minister, while the Head of State is the Queen of England, who is represented here by a resident Governor-General.

FOOD AND DRINK

Kiwi cooking is distinguished by ingredients that are fresh and flavourful, and a style that fuses a medley of influences, reflecting the country's cultural diversity. A latecomer to the world of wine-making, it now also produces outstanding vintages that are sold and acclaimed worldwide.

Above: kiwifruit; crayfish is a delicacy.

Cooking Class
If tasting the delights of New Zealand cuisine isn't enough, you can also learn to cook the Kiwi way. Cooking classes are becoming popular, and courses include Catherine Bell's Epicurean Workshop in Auckland and Ruth Pretty's Wellington countryside school, both of which attract foodies from far and wide.

Fresh and vibrant, New Zealand's cuisine is often described as Pacific Rim, as it draws much of its inspiration from Europe, Asia and Polynesia. This blend of influences has created a mouthwatering range of flavours and food that can be sampled in cafés, restaurants and lodges nationwide. Innovative chefs make clever use of tasty ingredients freshly harvested from the garden, land and sea – which, in the company of award-winning local wines, make the New Zealand gastronomic experience among the best in the world.

While food and beverage production has long been the linchpin of New Zealand's prosperity and a leading export earner, it's the fusion of unique, quality produce and ethnic influences that has allowed a national food identity to evolve. Nowadays New Zealand's worldwide reputation for award-winning produce draws visitors from afar to the source, and food tourism is developing at a rapid rate.

TRADITIONAL DINING

The country's cuisine culture is also distinctive in the way that New Zealanders prefer to eat; an environment that is as relaxed and unaffected as possible, in tune with the laid-back Kiwi psyche.

Summer usually means endless barbecues and alfresco dining, with the emphasis on fresh, simple fare. Barbecues have long been a big part of the Kiwi culture, and Pacific influences, organic or home-grown produce, and indigenous foods make it unique. Fare such as lamb, venison, fresh fish including crayfish (lobster) and other shellfish such as pipi, tuatua and scallops, are fresh-harvested and plentiful.

The Hangi

For an authentic New Zealand eating experience, try a traditional Maori *hangi* (pronounced 'hung-ee'), cooked underground. A deep hole is dug, then lined with red-hot stones and covered with vegetation. The food (chicken, pork, lamb, potatoes, kumara – sweet potato – and other vegetables) is placed on top, then the whole 'oven' is sprinkled with water and sealed, and left to steam for several hours, giving a smoky taste.

Traditionally, all members of a *whanau* (family) come for the feast, with stereotypical gender roles the norm: the men digging and working on the hole, and the women preparing the food to go in it. Several tourist locations, including Rotorua in the North Island, invite visitors to join in and experience *hangi* culture (see p.53).

SEAFOOD

Fish is abundant and of very good quality in New Zealand, with varieties including freshwater salmon, sole and flounder. If you want to eat trout, however, note that you will have to catch your own, as it is illegal to sell it *(see p.57)*. A seasonal delicacy is inanga (whitebait), a tiny minnow-like fish, that can be enjoyed nationwide, although it has become synonymous with the South Island's West Coast.

On your travels, look out for roadside stalls selling succulent crayfish and/or freshly smoked mussels or fish. The sublime flavour of crayfish can also be enjoyed at any good seafood restaurant; try White Morph (Kaikoura, South Island) or Harbourside Seafood Bar & Grill (Quay Street, Auckland).

Throughout the year, shellfish such as mussels, pipi and tuatua can be gathered freely from the beach. Green-lipped mussels, paua (abalone) and oysters – the Pacific oyster, the rock oyster and the famed Bluff oyster – can also be found on menus nationwide.

British visitors may be pleased to learn that fish and chips are a popular takeaway meal in New Zealand, served in the traditional way: piping hot and wrapped in paper.

NATIONAL SPECIALITIES

Your New Zealand culinary experience is incomplete until you savour the sweet, creamy stickiness of pavlova, the national dessert. In addition, it's worth looking out for some food products that offer an entirely new taste sensation. These include hokey pokey ice cream (vanilla ice cream with toffee bits in it),

Above from far left: New Zealand lamb; mussels; delicatessen fare; fresh salmon.

Markets
Many New Zealanders do part of their main weekly shop at their local farmers' market, making the most of reasonably priced seasonal produce and home-made preserves. Hand-made cheeses, artisan breads, natural ice cream, hand-crafted chocolates, gourmet meats and organic coffee are also often up for grabs.

Below: market-fresh organic produce.

Above: Hokitika is known for its annual Wild Foods Festival, although it's not for the faint-hearted.

L&P soft drink (short for 'Lemon and Paeroa', a lemon-flavoured sparkling drink), tamarillos (tree tomatoes) and feigoas (fruit), and 'chocolate' fish.

Indigenous treats include kumara, a type of sweet potato commonly eaten throughout New Zealand and an essential part of any Sunday roast, Rewena and Takakau bread, piko piko pesto, and huhu grubs, the latter found in backyards nationwide, but usually only served at local wild foods festivals.

FOOD FESTIVALS

Food festivals are regularly held throughout the nation, but when it comes to wild cuisine, there's no better place to start than Hokitika. This West Coast town leads the way in untamed gastronomic creativity, with all manner of culinary delights up for grabs during the annual Wild Foods Festival, held to celebrate the harvest.

Stallholders provide crowds with a variety of bizarre tucker, from crickets and huhu grubs to bull's penis and pig's ears and even worm sushi. The less adventurous are not forgotten, however, with gourmet treats such as rabbit pâté, pickled seaweed, ostrich pie, crayfish, whitebait and home-made ice cream also available.

Wine and food festivals are held annually in Auckland, Bay of Islands, Coromandel, Hawke's Bay, Martin-borough, Blenheim, Canterbury and Queenstown. These national and regional events highlight the produc-tion of a wide-ranging supply of gourmet foods and boutique wines.

WINE

Needless to say, New Zealand wines are the only complement to the local cuisine that visitors should consider during their stay. It all began at the top of the country in the Bay of Islands, with James Busby, official British Resident, horticulturist extraordinaire, pioneer viticulturist (he also founded the wine industry in New South Wales, Australia) and author of the Treaty of Waitangi. He planted the first vineyard on his property at Wait-angi in the Bay of Islands in 1833, and a couple of years later the very first New Zealand wine was produced. It was sampled by French admiral Dumont d'Urville, who pronounced it to be light, sparkling and delicious.

From that point forward the history of wine-making in New Zealand becomes obscure. However, it is known that early French settlers planted small vineyards at Akaroa (South Island) and Marist Brothers established a winery at Mission Estate (www.missionestate.co.nz) in Hawke's Bay in 1865. This is still operating and is now a commercial venture, making it New Zealand's oldest vineyard.

By the end of the century, small commercial vineyards were established in other parts of Hawke's Bay and in the Auckland-Northland region. However, vineyards country-wide suffered and the wine industry was effectively destroyed by the scourge of prohibition politics between 1900 and 1920. Fortunately the industry is now thriving with several distinct wine-growing regions, each with its own

wine trail. Many vineyards offer a cellar door experience.

International Standing

If New Zealand has a signature wine, it is sauvignon blanc, but pinot noir is also in the running. To sample fruity, fresh-scented sauvignon blancs from a range of award-winning vineyards, head to the notoriously sunny valleys of the Marlborough region (www.wine-marlborough.co.nz). Pinot noir has placed the southern North Island wine growing region of the Wairarapa (www.wairarapanz.com) firmly on the map, and other varietals including syrah (known in Australia and New Zealand as shiraz) and pinot gris are steadily increasing in popularity.

PLACES TO EAT

Most major towns and cities have a range of eateries, from food courts to cafés, casual restaurants and brasseries, through to high-class establishments. Like everything, you will get what you pay for, but it is fair to say that there is a trend towards a lighter and healthier style of cooking, with a focus on fresh New Zealand produce. Likewise, cafés are increasingly replacing the tearooms of old. Most restaurants/cafés offer at least one or two vegetarian and/or gluten-free dishes on their menu.

Cafés open as early as 7am, while most restaurants tend to commence service around 6pm, with last orders taken around 10pm. Note that in smaller towns it's best to book, as restaurants will close early – or not open at all – if they think they have no patrons.

Many restaurants are licensed, and BYO (Bring Your Own) places – licensed for the consumption and not the sale of alcohol – are also popular. Feel free to take along bottles of wine, but note that bringing your own beer is frowned upon.

Above from far left: fresh, light food is fashionable; on the Hawke's Bay wine trail; dining alfresco at Huka Lodge *(see p.115).*

Below: New Zealand is famous for its sauvignon blanc.

SHOPPING

Trade in your New Zealand dollars for, among other things, hand-crafted Maori carvings, pretty jade and iridescent paua-shell jewellery, hand-made pottery and, of course, woolly jumpers and sheepskin goods.

Above: pretty *paua* shell; pottery jandals (flip-flops).

Walk of Fame
At Victoria Park Market look out for the Celebrity Walk of Fame, located on the old horse ramp that leads between the stable buildings and the courtyard. Here, the hand (or footprints) of New Zealand's most outstanding modern-day achievers, including Sir Edmund Hillary, Dame Kiri Te Kanawa and comedian Billy T. James, are immortalised in cement.

New Zealand offers a huge variety of shopping from arts and craft markets, gallery and museum shops to exclusive designer stores. For traditional New Zealand souvenirs look for hand-crafted Maori carvings in wood, bone and *pounamu* (greenstone or jade). You can also find jewellery and ornaments made from the iridescent *paua* shell (abalone), treasured by Maori for centuries.

New Zealand potters are among the world's finest, and today many artisans are also working in stone, wood, glass and metals. With over 40 million sheep, it is no surprise that the country's wool industry is going strong; wonderful hand-knitted wool sweaters, beautiful wall hangings, homespun yarns and top-quality sheepskins are plentiful. New Zealand also has 70 million possums (culled as this introduced species is damaging to the environment), so expect to see possum-skin goods, too.

Alongside top international fashion in the main city areas, you will also find New Zealand's own fashion labels, including Zambesi, NomD, Karen Walker and World.

New Zealanders love the great outdoors, so it should come as little surprise that they have developed a wide range of hard-wearing clothing and equipment to match tough environmental demands. Warm and rugged farm-wear such as Swanndri bush shirts and jackets are popular purchases, while mountaineering equipment, camping gear and backpacks set world standards. Some items have even become fashion success stories, such as the Canterbury range of rugby and yachting jerseys.

WHERE TO BUY

Auckland

New Zealand's largest city offers some of the country's most varied retail therapy. Queen Street is the hub for souvenir shopping, with 'downtown' Queen Street hosting the major duty-free stores. For a full range of items, try the DFS Galleria on the corner of Customs Street and Albert Street. Vulcan Lane, off Queen Street, leads to High Street and the Chancery District, where Auckland's major designer fashion boutiques are clustered. The wares of up-and-coming designers can be found in the city fringe suburbs of Ponsonby and Parnell.

For a completely different shopping experience, go to Victoria Park Market (daily 9am–6pm), recognisable by its large red-brick chimney, on Victoria

Street West, where a huge variety of goods from leatherware through to pottery is on offer; there are cafés in the complex, too.

Rotorua

The main shopping street in Rotorua is Tutanekai Street, although several souvenir shops are on Fenton Street, close to the Visitor Centre. Maori arts and crafts abound here, as do leather and sheepskin products. The Best of Maori Tourism (1189 Fenton Street) offers original Maori-designed clothing and carvings in bone and wood. Craftspeople can be watched while they work at The Jade Factory (1288 Fenton Street), and at Te Puia, the New Zealand Maori Arts and Crafts Institute at Whakarewarewa on Hemo Road.

Wellington

Shopping in the capital city centres around Lambton Quay and ranges from high-street chains such as Farmers, to clothing chain stores such as Country Road and Max. Bookstores including Whitcoulls and Dymocks are good places to pick up holiday reading.

For crafts and antiques, spend an hour or two browsing the converted villas of Tinakori Road. If you prefer less mainstream fashions, the small designer clothing stores that compete for space with second-hand bookshops along Cuba Street are recommended. Also worth a visit is Wellington institution Kirkaldie and Staines; located at 165–77 Lambton Quay, this department store is renowned for its quality products and good old-fashioned service.

Queenstown

Queenstown aims to please its visitors in every way possible – including shopping – with many stores open for extended hours on a daily basis, so you can buy just about anything, at any time.

Jewellery, duty-free and artisan stores line The Mall, while O'Connells Shopping Centre, at the corner of Camp Street and Beach Street, hosts around 25 stores under one roof, including New Zealand's largest Canterbury of New Zealand store. It sells a wide range of All Blacks and rugby-inspired clothing.

Queenstown's focus on outdoor pursuits is strongly reflected in its wealth of high-quality sportswear apparel and equipment shops, which can be found all over town *(see margin tip, right)*.

PRACTICALITIES

The majority of shops and businesses open 9am to 5pm, Monday to Friday, but many stores also open on Saturday and Sunday, especially in the large cities. In resort areas, too, you will find shops open in the evenings, until around 9pm.

It's worth noting that in a few shops you may experience problems if your credit card uses 'Smart Card' technology; contact your card provider for further information prior to travelling to New Zealand.

Above from far left: traditional Maori textile; detail of a sheepskin rug; carved jade pendant with woven bag.

Bookstores

Bookworms will be right at home in New Zealand as the nation has more bookshops per head of population than any other country in the world – one for every 7,500 people.

ENTERTAINMENT

In the past, many Kiwis found it necessary to relocate overseas to move their talents and careers forward; not so these days. Those who have made it big at home have inspired a whole new level of confidence in Kiwi creativity.

Listings

To find out what's on, check the entertainment pages of local newspapers or visit www.nzlive.com, a site dedicated to New Zealand culture online. You can book on this site by following the links, or alternatively, most major events can be booked through Ticketek (www.ticketek.co.nz). Other publications that list entertainment details include the monthly *Theatre News*, *NZ Musician*, *Music in New Zealand*, *Rip it Up*, *Real Groove* and *Pulp* magazines, all of which are available at major newsagents.

New Zealanders have always interpreted the world in unexpected ways and exploring its entertainment scene opens the door to a whole new world. It's a landscape formed by a blend of influences, a kaleidoscope of Maori, Samoan, Pacific Island, European and Asian cultures. From film-makers and performers, to writers, designers and musicians, each has helped to evolve New Zealand's performing arts, which are incredibly strong for a small Pacific Island nation with limited funding.

THEATRE

Maori and Pacific Island writers and performers have provided New Zealand's theatre with a unique and colourful Polynesian-influenced identity. Theatre companies such as Wellington's Taki Rua (tel: 04 385 3110; www.takirua.co.nz) and the Auckland Theatre Company (tel: 09 309 0390; www.atc.co.nz) both stage local plays. However, it's the Court Theatre in Christchurch (tel: 03 963 0870; www.courttheatre.org.nz) that is regarded as New Zealand's leading theatre, with a small, high-quality ensemble and international guest actors performing middle-of-the-road modern drama. Smaller venues producing edgier works in Auckland

include Silo (tel: 09 366 0339; www.silotheatre.co.nz) and Depot Arts Space (tel: 09 963 2331; http://depotartspace.co.nz). Daring and inspired works can be seen at Wellington's Bats (tel: 04 802 4176; www.bats.co.nz).

DANCE

Dance has always played a major role in Maori culture and Kapa Haka (performance dances) is an integral part of daily life in New Zealand; the best groups tour internationally to share this unique form of cultural art. The Royal New Zealand Ballet is well worth seeing, along with a plethora of contemporary dance companies including Auckland's Black Grace Dance Company which performs worldwide *(see margin, right)* and Wellington's Footnote Dance Company.

MUSIC

Unexpectedly, given its size, New Zealand has three professional symphony orchestras, including the New Zealand Symphony Orchestra (NZSO), and several choirs including the National Youth Choir, which regularly wins international events. Recent co-productions between the Royal New Zealand Ballet, NZSO, and

Maori music and dance groups have showcased New Zealand's contemporary bi-cultural 'fusion'. Meanwhile, the modern and alternative music scene is diverse. Rapper Pauly Fuemana of OMC fame and Crowded House's Neil Finn are New Zealand's best-known musicians, but performers such as Bic Runga, Stellar, Shihad and King Kapisi are also making waves, along with classical singing sensation Hayley Westenra.

FILM

Building upon cultural icon Peter Jackson's *Lord of the Rings* trilogy, indigenous film projects have, in recent times, been hugely successful. Director Nicky Caro followed her international hit *Whale Rider* with *In My Father's Den*, a favourite at international film festivals. Other New Zealand directors turning heads include Taika Waititi *(Two Cars, One Night)* and Andrew Adamson *(Prince Caspian)*. It's fitting that Peter Jackson's home town of Wellington has more screens per capita than anywhere else in New Zealand; among these is The Embassy Theatre, the city's grandest.

NIGHTLIFE

New Zealand's nightlife is, by international standards, limited, and really only exists in major cities. Most small towns boast only a pub but main cities offer a variety of dance clubs and late-night bars. Auckland's offerings include Caluzzi on K' Road, The Dog's Bollix

on Newton Road, and Ponsonby Road's Chapel Bar. Meanwhile, Wellington's Courtney Place pumps with Hummingbird and Boogie Wonderland, with Bodega just around the corner on Ghuznee Street.

FESTIVALS

While New Zealand's nightlife may be tame, its festivals are rather wacky. Highlights include The World of Wearable Art Awards in Wellington; Christchurch's World Buskers Festival; Hokitika's Wild Foods Festival; Napier's Art Deco Weekend and Taihape's Gumboot Day. However, the most significant celebration is Waitangi Day, when the signing of New Zealand's founding document, The Treaty of Waitangi, is celebrated nationwide.

Above from far left: a Kapa Haka; 70s-themed club Boogie Wonderland.

Black Grace Auckland's all-male dance company, Black Grace, features some of New Zealand's most respected contemporary dancers (tel: 09 358 0552; www.black grace.co.nz).

Below: a Royal New Zealand Ballet performance of *Don Quixote*.

HISTORY: KEY DATES

From early days as a Polynesian settlement and the arrival of the Maori to European rule and, finally, independence. The list below covers important social and political events in the history of New Zealand.

Woodcarving
The New Zealand forests contained larger trees than Polynesians would previously have seen. This enabled them to build bigger-than-ever dugout canoes and resulted in a fine tradition of woodcarving.

Early Tourism
The North Island's spas and hot pools earned an early reputation for their curative powers. As early as 1901, the government hired an official balneologist and formed a tourist department, the first government-sponsored tourism promotion organisation in the world.

DISCOVERY

800	First Polynesian settlers.
1642	Discovery by Abel Tasman.
1769	Captain James Cook's first exploration of New Zealand.

19TH CENTURY

1814	Reverend Samuel Marsden establishes an Anglican mission station.
1826	Attempt at European settlement under Captain Herd.
1840	Treaty of Waitangi is signed by 50 Maori chiefs. Arrival of New Zealand Company's settlers in Wellington.
1841	New Zealand proclaimed independent of New South Wales.
1844	'Northern War' between Maori and *Pakeha* (Europeans).
1852	Constitution Act passed. New Zealand divided into six provinces.
1853	The Maori King movement, designed to protect tribal land, begins.
1854	First session of the General Assembly in Auckland.
1860	'Taranaki War' between *Pakeha* and Maori when land is confiscated.
1861	Gold discovery in Otago. First electric telegraph line opens.
1863	First steam railway opens.
1865	Seat of government transferred to Wellington from Auckland.
1867	Maori are given the vote.
1870	New Zealand's first rugby match. Last battles of 'New Zealand Wars'.
1876	Provincial governments abolished.
1882	First shipment of frozen meat from New Zealand.
1886	Mount Tarawera erupts.
1893	Universal female suffrage is introduced.

20TH CENTURY

1907	The country is granted Dominion status.
1908	North Island main trunk railway opens. Ernest Rutherford awarded Nobel Prize for Chemistry.
1914–18	World War I. Gallipoli campaign by ANZAC troops.

1918	Influenza epidemic.
1931	Hawke's Bay earthquake.
1935	First New Government elected (Labour).
1939–45	World War II. New Zealand Division serves in Italy.
1947	Statute of Westminster adopted by Parliament.
1949	National Party wins the general election.
1951	Prolonged waterfront industrial dispute. New Zealand signs ANZUS Treaty alliance with US and Australia.
1953	Sir Edmund Hillary successfully climbs Mount Everest.
1965	Troops sent to Vietnam.
1972	Labour Government elected.
1974	Christchurch hosts the Commonwealth Games.
1975	Waitangi Tribunal established to hear Maori land-rights issues. National Party elected.
1981	Tour of New Zealand by South African rugby team leads to riots.
1983	Closer Economic Relations (CER) agreement with Australia.
1984	Labour Government elected. New Zealand becomes nuclear-free.
1985	Greenpeace protest vessel *Rainbow Warrior* bombed by French agents in Auckland.
1990	Auckland hosts the Commonwealth Games. National Party wins general election.
1993	Electoral system changed to a proportional system called MMP.
1994	New Zealand wins America's Cup yachting regatta in San Diego.
1995	Waikato's Tainui tribe settles a long-standing grievance claim.
1996	First MMP election. National Party forms coalition government with a minor party, New Zealand First.
1999	New Zealand hosts APEC summit and America's Cup yachting regatta. Labour Party coalition wins the election.

21ST CENTURY

2003	Team New Zealand loses the America's Cup in Auckland. The population reaches 4 million.
2004	The film *The Lord of the Rings: The Return of the King* wins all 11 Academy Awards for which it was nominated.
2007	Sir Edmund Hillary passes away. The nation goes into mourning.
2008	National Party elected. John Key becomes Prime Minister.
2010	Magnitude 7.1 earthquake rocks Christchurch. Pike River Mine disaster claims lives of 29 coal miners.
2011	Shallow magnitude 6.3 earthquake centred in Christchurch claims 172 lives. New Zealand hosts Rugby World Cup.

Above from far left: signing the Treaty of Waitangi; driving sheep in the 1920s.

Women's Rights
New Zealand has always taken pride in the fact that in 1893 it became the first country in the world to give women the vote, and at the start of the 21st century the prominence of women in public life suggested a developed degree of equality. Arguably the three top positions in the country – Prime Minister, Governor-General and Chief Justice – have been held by women; the second-, third- and fifth-biggest cities have had women mayors; and the chief executive officers of the two major telecommunications companies and biggest bank were women. However, statistics indicate that the median wage for women remains lower than that enjoyed by men.

WALKS AND TOURS

The North Island

1. Auckland   26
2. Around Auckland   33
3. Northland   36
4. Coromandel Peninsula   42
5. Tauranga District   46
6. Rotorua   49
7. Taupo   54
8. Wellington   60
9. The Wairarapa   65

The South Island

10. Ferry to the South Island   68
11. Dunedin and Otago Peninsula   71
12. Akaroa   76
13. Hanmer Springs   80
14. Christchurch to Queenstown   83
15. Arthur's Pass and West Coast   86
16. Queenstown   92
17. Arrowtown   95
18. Milford Sound   98

AUCKLAND

The country's largest city sits between the harbours of Waitemata and Manukau on an isthmus dotted with extinct volcanoes. This walking tour takes in its key sights, including Auckland Domain, Parnell and the Sky Tower.

Harbour Bridge

The Auckland Harbour Bridge opened on 30 May 1959. The construction took 200 workers, around four years, 6,500 tonnes of concrete and nearly 6,000 tonnes of steel. A few years later 'clippons' (made in Japan) were added to cope with the increasing volume of traffic; they were attached with huge steel pins and rods. To explore the length and breadth of the bridge, take a Bridgeclimb (Westhaven Reserve; tel: 09 360 7748; www. aucklandbridgeclimb. co.nz; daily; charge), which offers an optional bungy jump on the way down.

DISTANCE 7km (4½ miles)
TIME A full day
START Viaduct Harbour
END Sky Tower
POINTS TO NOTE

There is much ground to cover on this route, and you can take bus or taxi rides between key points of interest to spare your feet and save some time along the way, if you want. Another option is to board the Auckland Explorer Bus (tel: 09 524 7929 or 0800 439 756; www.explorerbus.co.nz; charge), a hop-on/hop-off tour featuring many of the sights on this and the next tour. The bus departs from the Ferry Building on Quay Street and runs hourly from 9am throughout the day.

Sandwiched between twin harbours and built on 53 extinct volcanoes, Auckland has long been New Zealand's prime gateway and largest city. Its population topped 1 million a few years ago, and growth is proceeding at a pace that indicates it will reach 2 million by the year 2036. Auckland has the largest Polynesian population of any city in the world; it also has a growing Asian presence, currently about 12 percent. Scenic areas such as the Waitakere Ranges to the west, the Hunua Ranges to the south, and Waiwera and Puhoi to the north will be maintained as green belts and therefore protected from development.

City of Sails

To the west of Auckland are the shallow waters of the Manukau Harbour, navigable only to small ships. The Waitemata Harbour to the east is a 'Sea of Sparkling Water', indented with bays and scattered with islands. One of them, Rangitoto, an active volcano until just 200 years ago, stands guard at the harbour entrance (for more on Rangitoto, *see tour 2, p.33*).

To the Maori people, the area was *Tamaki-makau-rau*, 'the place of a hundred lovers'. British administrators renamed it, rather less poetically, after an English admiral. Auckland has long since dropped its colonial sobriquet of 'Queen City' and now prefers 'City of Sails'. It is said to possess the world's highest number of boats per head of population, and it certainly looks that way each January, during the Anniversary Day yachting regatta, the world's largest one-day event. The race celebrates the foundation of the city in 1840 as capital of the country – a title it lost 25 years later to Wellington.

VIADUCT HARBOUR

This tour of the city begins downtown at the **Viaduct Harbour** ❶, where **Mecca**, see ⓘⓘ, is a good place for breakfast. After strolling along the waterfront, exit the harbour at the Quay Street archway, where a large suspended yacht, a legacy of New Zealand's endeavours in the America's Cup regatta, is on display. For a taste of America's Cup action, pop into Sail NZ (Viaduct Harbour; tel: 09 359 5987; www.sailingnz.co.nz), which organises thrilling trips aboard *NZL40*

Above from far left: the city by night; racing yachts at full speed near Auckland.

Food and Drink

① MECCA
85–7 Customs Street West, Viaduct Harbour; tel: 09 358 1093; $$
Modern Mediterranean-influenced cuisine, with tasty breakfasts and excellent coffee. Indoor and outdoor seating, and harbour views.

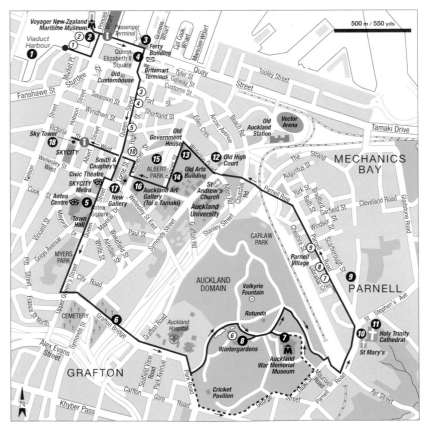

Formal Gardens

The Auckland Domain's Formal Gardens evolved in the 1860s on a site on which the Auckland Acclimatisation Society tested and propagated exotic trees, birds and trout. Its duck ponds were the source, in 1866, of Auckland's first piped water supply.

and *NZL41*. Take the helm, give it a blast on the grinders or just sit back and enjoy the sights.

Maritime Museum

For an insight into New Zealand's maritime history, check out the nearby **Voyager New Zealand Maritime Museum ❷** (Princes Wharf; tel: 09 373 0800; www.maritimemuseum.co.nz; daily 9am–5pm; charge), just by the waterfront. The museum showcases boats of all types and is home to **The Waterfront Café & Bar**, see ⑪②. Fifteen-minute trips around the harbour aboard the historic steamboat SS *Puke* and 2½-hour trips on the traditional sailing ship SS *Breeze* depart sporadically from here. Trips are posted on the website, under What's On, one month prior to departure.

Right: the yacht in front of the Maritime Museum is a legacy of the country's endeavours in the America's Cup yachting regatta.

Visitor Information Centre and Ferry Building

From the museum, take a stroll along the waterfront, passing the **Visitor Information Centre** (137 Quay Street, Princes Wharf; tel: 09 307 0614; Mon–Fri 8.30am–5.30pm, Sat–Sun 8.30am–5pm) en route to the historic **Ferry Building ❸** at 99 Quay Street. Erected in 1912 to house the offices of harbour officials, this red-brick edifice is now the focal point for commuter ferries that link Auckland with the North Shore and the islands of the Waitemata Harbour and Hauraki Gulf. (Board from the back of the building.)

QUEEN STREET

Cross Quay Street to the fully paved **Queen Elizabeth II Square ❹**, the home of the Britomart Train Terminus, one of the city's key public transport interchanges and the base of Queen Street, the city's main shopping area. Stroll along Queen Street, exploring side streets (home to pit stops including **Revive**, see ⑪③, and the **Vulcan Café**, see ⑪④) and eventually leading to the High Street, with boutique and designer stores and the fashionable **Vivace**, see ⑪⑤.

Further up on the right at 253–61 Queen Street, you will pass the department store **Smith & Caughey's** (tel: 09 377 4770; www.smithandcaughey.co.nz) and the historic **Civic Theatre** (corner of Queen Street and Wellesley Street; www.civictheatre.co.nz), which hosts many of Auckland's premier events. Just beyond is the SKYCITY

entertainment complex *(see p.32)*, where you can view the latest blockbusters or browse the books at Borders bookstore.

AOTEA SQUARE

The adjacent **Aotea Square** ❺ has several points of interest. The first is the elaborately carved Maori **Waharoa** (gateway). A symbolic entrance to the square, it stands in stark contrast to the surrounding mirrored-glass buildings. Across Aotea Square is Auckland's main cultural venue, **Aotea Centre** (tel: 09 309 2677; www.the-edge.co.nz). In the foyer you can find out about current and upcoming events, and purchase tickets. On Fridays and Saturdays between 10am and 6pm, the **Aotea Square Market** (tel: 09 309 2677) comes alive with stalls selling funky streetwear, jewellery, food and assorted bric-a-brac.

Bordering the square are City Council buildings, including the renovated **Town Hall**, recognisable by its angular form and the clock tower on the eastern fringe.

AUCKLAND DOMAIN

From here, the next destination is Auckland Domain, New Zealand's oldest park. To get there, you can walk, catch a bus (the Link bus from Queen Street) or hail a taxi. This journey of about 1km (½ mile) will take you over **Grafton Bridge** ❻ and past Auckland Hospital into **Auckland Domain** (daily 24 hours; Wintergardens: *see p.30*), New Zealand's oldest park and the site of a huge volcanic explosion that took place thousands of years ago. The wide crater has formed a natural amphitheatre arching from the hospital to the Auckland War Memorial Museum *(see below)* and is the venue of numerous outdoor sporting and cultural events. If you are arriving by taxi, ask the driver to point out the Wintergardens and Sugar & Spice Café *(see p.30 and p.31)* along the way. If you are on foot, head into the park from Park Road. If you are on the bus, get off on Parnell Road, slightly further southeast.

Auckland War Memorial Museum
The main sight in the park, the imposing **Auckland War Memorial Museum** ❼ (tel: 09 309 0443; www.aucklandmuseum.com; daily 10am–5pm; charge), enjoys a prime location with panoramic views of the Domain and parts of the city and harbour.

All Blacks
Success in rugby is synonymous with New Zealand's All Blacks. For information on tickets to games, the history of the team and even the lowdown on the *haka* (the Maori dance performed prior to each game) visit www.allblacks.com.

Food and Drink

② THE WATERFRONT CAFÉ & BAR
Maritime Museum Building, Viaduct Harbour; tel: 09 359 9914; $
The Maritime Museum's café has a broad European-style menu and does great late breakfasts.

③ REVIVE
16 Fort Street; tel: 09 307 1586; $
Tasty and nutritious vegetarian fare, much of which is organic.

④ VULCAN CAFÉ
19 Vulcan Lane; tel: 09 377 9899; $$
The Vulcan Café is slap-bang in the middle of this designer shopping area. The Cajun chicken salad is highly recommended.

⑤ VIVACE
50 High Street; tel: 09 302 2302; $
Italian-style food and a selection of hot and cold tapas, accompanied by an excellent wine list. Lunch and dinner only.

Museum Library
Formed in 1867, the Auckland War Memorial Museum Library is one of the major research libraries in New Zealand, and has expanded to include rare collections of books, maps, manuscripts and archives relating in particular to Auckland, New Zealand and the South Pacific.

Local Volcanoes
Auckland's volcanoes first began to appear between 60,000 and 140,000 years ago, starting with the eruptions of the Domain and Albert Park. The largest and most recent eruption was Rangitoto, which occurred around 600 years ago.

The museum was constructed in 1929 and provides an excellent overview of the natural, cultural and social history of New Zealand. For the first-time visitor it also provides a superb introduction to Maori culture through its collection of artefacts, including a raised storehouse, a carved meeting house and, possibly the most spectacular exhibit, *Te Toki a Tapiri*, a great Maori war canoe carved from a single totara log. This 25m (82ft) long boat was built in 1836 to seat approximately 100 warriors. There are daily performances featuring traditional Maori song and dance, and the 'Scars on the Heart' display depicts the compelling story of New Zealand at war.

As you walk around the museum, keep an eye out for Auckland's most revered volcanic peaks. These include: **One Tree Hill**, once topped by a lone summit pine but now marked only by an obelisk; **Mount Eden**; and the slopes of **Rangitoto Island** *(see p.35)*. Note the names of locations etched in the stone around the entire museum facade: these were the battlefields where New Zealanders were killed in overseas wars in the 20th century.

The Wintergardens

There is a café in the museum, but there's also a treat in store if you walk from the front of the museum back down to the **Sugar & Spice Café**, see ⑪⑥. On the south side of the teahouse, a takeaway kiosk (daily 9am–5pm) sells ice creams and other snacks.

If time permits, take a stroll behind the tearooms through the **Winter-**gardens ❽ (Apr–Oct daily 9am–4.30pm, Nov–Mar Mon–Sat 9am–5.30pm, Sun 9am–7.30pm; free), a conservatory housing some 10,000 exotic plants. Look out for the short native bush walk, which gives an indication of the type of vegetation still covering large tracts of the countryside.

PARNELL

From the Wintergardens, follow the path that runs southeast around the perimeter of the Domain and out to Parnell Road. Turn left here and take a 15-minute walk to **Parnell** ❾, a vibrant inner-city suburb known for its boutique shopping and wide range of eateries, such as **Trinity Café**, see ⑪⑦.

As you walk, look out, on your right, for **St Mary's Church** ❿ *(see margin, right)*, regarded as one of the finest wooden Gothic buildings in New Zealand, and for the **Holy Trinity Cathedral** ⓫, which was completed only in 1995.

Just 30m/yds further, at the St Stephen's Avenue intersection, is a mix of bakeries, 'dairies' (small grocery stores), fish-and-chip shops and the start of the designer shops that become more apparent as you venture down the hill. Another good pit stop at this point is the **Strawberry Alarm Clock**, see ⑪⑧.

The Parnell Village complex on the left-hand side of Parnell Road comprises characterful wooden villas reclaimed and restored for retail purposes. Walk around the verandas and over the little bridges linking villa to villa

to access the shops. For lunch and to watch the world go by, get a seat under the awning at **Verve Café**, see ⑪⑨.

BACK TO THE CENTRE

After pounding the pavements of Parnell, either hail a taxi or enjoy a half-hour walk back to the city centre. Your ultimate destination, on the corner of Federal and Victoria streets, is the landmark Sky Tower *(see p.32)*, which offers unparalleled views over the city, the Waitakere Ranges and the gulf islands.

If you're on foot, veer left down Parnell Rise. Once at the bottom, walk under the rail bridge and cross the Grafton motorway extension, then take a deep breath before tackling the hill on the other side. A path leads from Churchill Road up through a reserve area to the junction of Symonds Street and Alten Road, to the Romanesque columns of the Presbyterian **St Andrew's Church**. Directly opposite the church are the lower grounds of **Auckland University**.

High Court

Cross over, head west along the Waterloo Quadrant and, on your right, you will see the old **High Court ⑫**, with its historic chamber and court-rooms joined to a modern extension. Work started on the old Court building in 1865, and the first sitting took place three years later. The carved stone heads and gargoyles adorning its exterior were crafted by Anton Teutenburg, a Prussian immigrant who was paid 15 shillings a day for the task.

Old Government House

Moving on, you will see, on the left-hand side, at 12 Princes Street, the **Old Government House ⑬**, completed in 1856 and the former residence of the Governor-General of New Zealand. Cross the road to the entrance and take a stroll through the grounds, now owned by Auckland University. The building appears to be stone but is in fact clad entirely in kauri, a tall coniferous tree that once dominated New Zealand's landscape. Walk alongside the building and enjoy the lush subtropical gardens on the hillside leading up to Princes Street.

Old Arts Building

Make your way up Princes Street, where on the left you will see the **Old Arts Building ⑭**, designed and built

Above from far left: statues in the Wintergardens; the marina; smart town houses in Parnell.

St Mary's Church A church dedicated to St Mary has served Parnell parish since 1860. The present church was built between 1886 and 1897 on land opposite the cathedral. It was moved and rotated into its present position, with much controversy, in 1982.

Food and Drink 🍴

⑥ SUGAR & SPICE CAFÉ
Auckland Domain; tel: 09 303 0627; $
A lovely setting for tea, with views over duck ponds and the meandering walkways of the Domain. Open for lunch, and morning and afternoon tea.

⑦ TRINITY CAFÉ
107 Parnell Road; tel: 09 300 3042; $
Sleek, tasteful and comfortable café, doing great breakfasts and brunches. A good spot to people-watch on the busy Parnell Road.

⑧ STRAWBERRY ALARM CLOCK
119 Parnell Road; tel: 09 377 6959; $
This is an unpretentious, laid-back venue, with an enticing range of paninis and brunch dishes. Try the CLAT, a stacked sandwich of chicken, lettuce, avocado and tomato.

⑨ VERVE CAFÉ
311 Parnell Road; tel: 09 379 2860; $$
The Verve Café is a relaxing spot with a nice decked area for alfresco dining/drinking. Classic café food.

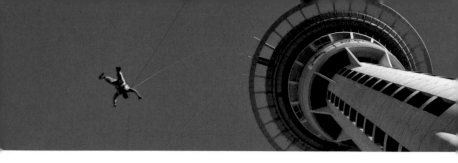

with the help of students from Auckland University College and opened in 1926. Locals call it the 'Wedding Cake', because of its ornate pinnacled white-stone construction.

Albert Park and Auckland Art Gallery

Opposite the Old Arts Building is **Albert Park** ⑮ (daily 24 hours), a beautifully maintained inner-city sanctum featuring a floral clock, statues of Queen Victoria and influential early colonial leader Sir George Grey (1812–98), a band rotunda and (usually) hordes of students lazing on the grass.

Now take one of the paths that lead downhill to Kitchener Street. On the corner of Wellesley Street is the **Auckland Art Gallery (Toi o Tamaki)** ⑯, heralded in 1888 as 'the first permanent art gallery in the Dominion'. Today, it is the country's largest art institution, with a collection of over 12,500 works, including New Zealand historic, modern and contemporary art, works by Maori and Pacific Island artists, and European paintings, sculpture and prints from 1376 to the present.

It is divided into two galleries. The **Main Gallery** (tel: 09 379 1349; www. aucklandartgallery.govt.nz; daily 10am–

5pm; free) displays mainly historical and European art collections, while the **New Gallery** ⑰ (corner of Wellesley and Lorne streets; tel: 09 379 1349; www. aucklandartgallery.govt.nz; daily 10am–5pm; free), which is accessed through a courtyard across the street, showcases cutting-edge contemporary art.

If you need refreshment, **Cima Café & Bar**, see ⑪⑩, is just to the west.

SKY TOWER

To end your exploration of the city centre, walk one block down Queen Street in the direction of the sea. This leads to Victoria Street, where you should turn left and walk up the slope to Auckland's most prominent landmark, the **Sky Tower** ⑱ (tel: 09 363 6000; www.skytower.co.nz; daily 8.30am–10pm, Fri–Sat until 10.30pm; charge for viewing decks). At 328m (1,076ft) high, it is the tallest tower in the southern hemisphere, offering breathtaking views for more than 80km (50 miles) – weather permitting.

If the heart-stopping elevator ride does not provide enough of an adrenaline rush, try the **Sky Jump** (Mission Control, Level 2, SKYCITY; tel: 0800 759 5867; www.skyjump.co.nz; daily 10am–5.15pm; charge), a wire-controlled 192m (630ft) leap from a platform near the viewing area.

SKYCITY

Adjacent is **SKYCITY** (tel: 09 363 6615; www.skycityauckland.co.nz; daily 24 hours), home to the Skycity casino, bars and entertainment areas.

Food and Drink 🍴
⑩ CIMA CAFÉ & BAR
56–8 High Street; tel: 09 303 1971; $
This espresso café and bar is good for a pick-me-up. To reach it from the Auckland Art Gallery, head north up Kitchener Street, west up Victoria Street, then right on to the High Street.

AROUND AUCKLAND

Spend a couple of hours driving around Auckland's waterfront, then catch a ferry either to historic Devonport and, time permitting, to the uninhabited Rangitoto Island, or to verdant Waiheke Island.

Among Auckland's attractions are its Waitemata (meaning 'sparkling') Harbour and surrounding bays. Popular with watersports fans, they also provide the focal point for this tour.

ALONG TAMAKI DRIVE

This drive begins at the landmark **Ferry Building ❶** *(see p.28)* at 99 Quay Street, then continues east along Quay Street, with the port to your left. Shortly after you pass the container terminal (on your left), Quay Street becomes Tamaki Drive. Hobson Bay is on your left at this point, and **Parnell Baths** (tel: 09 373 3561; Mon–Fri 6am–8pm, Sat–Sun 8am–8pm; charge), an outdoor swimming complex, are on your right. Beyond, across the harbour, the most prominent feature is the volcanic cone of the uninhabited **Rangitoto Island** *(see p.35)*, an optional visit for later.

Continuing along Tamaki Drive, following the signposts to St Heliers, you will pass **Okahu Bay**, the first of a string of city beaches. On your right is the broad, grassy area of **Orakei Domain**.

KELLY TARLTON'S

As you drive around the bay, watch out on the right for the Hammerheads seafood restaurant building; use it as

DISTANCE 21km (13 miles), excluding the island tours
TIME A full day
START/END Ferry Building, Auckland
POINTS TO NOTE

You will need a car in order to follow this tour to the letter; for details of car-hire firms, *see p.111* If you don't have a car, you could just follow the second part of the tour (ie the island visits). Remember to pack a bathing costume for the beach visits.

a landmark to move into the right-hand lane and turn into the car park at the well-signposted **Kelly Tarlton's Antarctic Encounter and Underwater World ❷** (23 Tamaki Drive; tel: 09 528 0603; www.kellytarltons.co.nz; daily 9.30am–5.30pm; charge). There's lots to see, including Auckland's latest high-adrenaline encounter with sharks in the 'Shark Cage'.

For a less watery experience, acrylic tunnels built under the sea take you through tanks of exotic New Zealand marine life. You can board a 'snow cat' to view penguins; the vehicles plunge through a 'white-out storm' to emerge in a re-created Antarctic landscape. Allow at least an hour and a half here.

Above: on the beach; driving through a vineyard on Waiheke Island; baby penguin at Kelly Tarlton's.

Above from left:
olive trees and vineyard on Waiheke Island; sunrise over the Hauraki Gulf; bird's-eye view of Devonport.

MISSION BAY

Resume your journey east for another 1km (½ mile) until you arrive at **Mission Bay ❸**. Turn left, off Tamaki Drive into either the first public car park or the second one near the large clock. Food-wise, there are lots of options, including **Otto Woo** and **Portofino**, see

Food and Drink

① OTTO WOO
Corner Tamaki Drive and Patteson Avenue, Mission Bay; tel: 09 521 8000; $
East meets West at this award-winning gourmet noodle bar.

② PORTOFINO
71 Tamaki Drive, Mission Bay; tel: 09 528 1212; $$
Family-owned Italian restaurant, well known for its traditional pizza and pasta dishes.

③ ANNABELLES
409 Tamaki Drive, St Heliers; tel: 09 575 5239; $$
Friendly, efficient staff serve a wide variety of seafood.

④ KAHVE
1 St Heliers Bay Road, St Heliers; tel: 09 575 2919; $
Delicious European fare served in an ambient, renovated 1920s store.

⑤ DEVONPORT STONE OVEN BAKERY AND CAFÉ
5 Clarence Street, Devonport; tel: 09 445 3185; $
Bakes 30 varieties of bread, all of which are fat-free and naturally fermented. Sourdough is a speciality. Good range of delicious cakes and pastries, plus excellent espressos.

⑥ VINO VINO
153 Ocean View Road, Oneroa, Waiheke Island; tel: 09 372 9888; $$
There are stunning views of Oneroa Bay from the deck of this popular café, where casual Mediterranean platters are served.

⑦ MUDBRICK CAFÉ
Church Bay Road, Waiheke Island; tel: 09 372 9050; $$$
The Mudbrick Café offers a winning combination of beautiful vineyard setting, varied menu, indoor and outdoor seating and great views of Auckland across the water.

🍴① and 🍴②, at the long line of eateries across the road from the beach. Alternatively, stock up on deli or bakery treats for a picnic on the lawn overlooking the beach; the spot by the fountain is a good choice for this. Afterwards, take a stroll along the promenade and perhaps take time out for a paddle.

Kohimarama and St Heliers

If you are feeling energetic, tackle the seaside walk east to **Kohimarama ❹**, 2km (1¼ miles) away, or to **St Heliers ❺**, a further 1km (½ mile), see 🍴③ and 🍴④. Every autumn (usually March), this route is filled with tens of thousands of people on the 'Round the Bays' fun run. Check the date on www.roundthebays.co.nz, if you want to avoid this.

Ladies Bay and Achilles Point

To continue the drive, head up Cliff Road at the end of Tamaki Drive to **Ladies Bay** and the lookout at **Achilles Point ❻**. Note the plaque honouring HMS *Achilles*, which took part in the 1939 Battle of the River Plate, then retrace your path along Tamaki Drive to the Ferry Building.

ISLAND TOURS

There are two recommendations for the rest of the day: a trip to Devonport and, time permitting, Rangitoto Island, or a trip to Waiheke Island. For both, take the ferry, leaving your car on the Auckland side (Fullers ferries only carry foot passengers). Note that the last ferry from Devonport to Rangitoto leaves at

12.15pm. (It is also possible to catch a ferry directly from Auckland to Rangitoto, but they only run at 9.15am and 10.30am, which makes them incompatible with the rest of this tour.)

Devonport and Rangitoto Island

Ferries for **Devonport** ❼ depart half-hourly from the Fullers Cruise Centre (Pier 1, Ferry Building, 99 Quay Street; tel: 09 367 9111; www.fullers.co.nz; daily 6am–11.30pm; charge); the crossing takes 12 minutes. Stroll up Victoria Street from the ferry terminal to the heart of the village. For information on sights, pop into the **Devonport i-Site Visitor Centre** (tel: 09 446 0677; daily 8.30am–5pm).

If the weather is good, consider hiking up the volcanic cones of **Mount Victoria** or **North Head** (check with the information centre for directions) for great harbour and gulf views, or visit Cheltenham Beach to relax and swim. Alternatively, browse Devonport's boutiques and antiques shops and relax at a café such as the **Devonport Stone Oven Bakery and Café**, see ⑪⑤.

If your timing is right, catch the 12.15pm ferry from Devonport to **Rangitoto Island** ❽ (the name means 'blood-red sky'). This 600-year-old volcano offers a mix of rugged lava outcrops and caves, lush native bush and sandy coves. Hike to the summit, which, at 260m (864ft), has spectacular views of Auckland and the Hauraki Gulf. Picnic beside the beach or hop aboard a four-wheel-drive volcanic explorer road train for a guided tour with Fullers (tel: 09 367 9111; www.fullers.co.nz; charge).

Waiheke Island

Another option is to visit **Waiheke Island** ❾ (ferries depart from Auckland's Ferry Building every hour with Fullers, half hourly during peak travel; journey time: 40 minutes). Waiheke has beautiful beaches, walking tracks, vineyards, native bush and laid-back seaside villages. Options for exploring include hiring a mountain bike, purchasing a hop-on, hop-off bus pass, or joining a 1½-hour Explorer Tour or Vineyard Tour through Fullers (tel: 09 367 9111; www.fullers.co.nz). Alternatively, take it easy at **Vino Vino** or the **Mudbrick Café**, see ⑪⑥ and ⑪⑦.

Devonport's Three Mounts

Devonport is located at the tip of a sandy beach-fringed peninsula that protrudes into the Waitemata Harbour. Fabulous 360-degree views over Auckland, the Waitemata Harbour and the islands of the Hauraki Gulf can be enjoyed from two of its 'Mounts'. Of these, Mount Victoria Takarunga is just a short hike away from where the ferry drops passengers at the wharf.

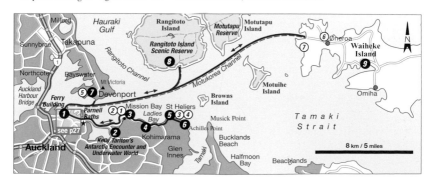

NORTHLAND

Kilometres of golden beaches, giant sand dunes, tranquil harbours, bush-clad islands and large tracts of ancient kauri forest are among the highlights on this driving tour of the North.

Scottish Links
Visitors to Waipu are greeted with signposts proclaiming in Celtic *Ceud Mile Failte* ('A hundred thousand welcomes'), reflecting the town's Scottish heritage: in the 1700s, some 900 hardy pioneers emigrated here. These links are celebrated at the annual Scottish games (country dancing and caber-tossing) on 1 and 2 January.

Above: tranquil fishing; thundering Whangarei Falls.

DISTANCE 977km (607 miles)
TIME Two to four days
START/END Auckland
POINTS TO NOTE
You will need a car for this tour; for details of car-hire firms, *see p.111*. Note, however, that hire cars are not insured on Ninety Mile Beach. For details of hotels in this area, *see p.113*.

Northland is often called the 'birthplace of the nation', thought to have been the landing point of the Maori adventurer Kupe in the 10th century; it was home to the first seat of government and was where the Treaty of Waitangi *(see pp.38–9)* was signed in 1840.

Along Northland's eastern edge is the Bay of Islands, known for its picturesque 800km (500-mile) coastline, which embraces 144 islands. At the northern tip of Northland is Cape Reinga, a place that is sacred to the Maori people *(see p.40)*. On the West Coast attractions include Hokianga, a sheltered harbour with a score of ragged inlets, and the fine Ninety Mile Beach.

TOWARDS WHANGAREI

Leaving **Auckland ❶** early via SH1, cross the Auckland Harbour Bridge, then continue on SH1, choosing the new toll route ($2; pay as indicated) following the signs to **Warkworth ❷**. For a breakfast stop, try **The Ginger Café**, see ⑪①, just under an hour from Auckland, or stretch your legs with a walk by the picturesque Mahurangi River.

Waipu and Whangarei

Driving another 100km (62 miles), past the small town of **Waipu ❸** (*see left*; also see ⑪②, if you need to stop) will bring you to Northland's main city (pop. 48,000) and erstwhile busy port, **Whangarei ❹**. As you enter on SH1, look out on the left for Tarewa Park, where there is an information centre.

If time allows, take a sidetrip to the **Whangarei Falls**, which plunge 25m (82ft) into a tranquil, bush-fringed pool. Hike the 20-minute walk around the falls before rejoining SH1.

BAY OF ISLANDS

Kawakawa

Now follow the signs to **Kawakawa ❺** (about one hour from Whangarei), which is part of the Bay of Islands, a maritime park of around 150 islands and bays *(see opposite)*. Highlights in Kawakawa township include the public toilets, which were transformed in 1999 by the Austrian artist Friedensreich

Hundertwasser *(see right)*. The toilets feature his trademark bright colours, organic forms and (most appropriate for this purpose) prolific use of tiles. For a meal in Kawakawa, try **The Platform Diner**, see ⑪③.

Paihia

At this point double back and turn off to **Paihia** ❻ via Opua. This busy little town offers plenty to do, and has many restaurants and hotels (see ⑪④ and ⑪⑤ and *p.114*); it is also the perfect departure point from which to explore the Bay of Islands. For more information, visit the Bay of Islands Information Office (Maritime Building, Paihia Wharf; tel: 09 402 7345; www.northlandnz.com; daily 8am–7pm), a circular building by the wharf.

History abounds here: Captain Cook and his crew sheltered among these islands in 1769 and gave the area its name; New Zealand's first colonists settled in nearby **Russell**, and it became the first capital; and New Zealand's founding document, the Treaty of Waitangi, was signed here in 1840.

Getting out onto the water is very tempting, and there is a huge range of day and half-day cruises and tours operated by Fullers Bay of Islands (Maritime Building, Paihia Wharf; tel: 09 402 7421; www.fboi.co.nz), including the Cape Brett/Hole in the Rock voyage, the Original Cream Trip, Tall Ship sailing, swimming with the dolphins and overnight cruises.

If time is short, we recommend prioritising the 'Hole in the Rock', the result of wind and sea erosion. For this,

hop aboard the *Excitor* (run by Fullers), or *Mack-Attack* (Maritime Building, Paihia; tel: 09 402 8180; www.mackattack.co.nz), a 90-minute blast to the Hole in a speedboat *(see p.38)*.

Russell

Most cruises offer the option of disembarking at **Russell** ❼. Set on a peninsula across the harbour, this quaint village is where New Zealand's first white colonialists settled. Local boat companies also provide a ferry service that crosses these waters every half-hour (journey time: 15 mins). Book at the Maritime Building or pay onboard.

Above from far left: fishing in the Bay; diving off the east coast of Northland; Ninety Mile Beach.

Friedensreich Hundertwasser
The Austrian-born artist (1928–2000) considered New Zealand to be his adopted home. Wherever he went in the world, he apparently kept his watch set at New Zealand time.

Food and Drink

① THE GINGER CAFÉ
21 Queen Street, Warkworth; tel: 09 422 2298; $
A popular bistro-style café serving wholesome fare including an excellent range of wheat-free, dairy-free and gluten-free options.

② WAIPU CAFÉ & DELI
29 The Centre, Waipu; tel: 09 432 0990; $
Freshly prepared sandwiches, rolls and panini and decent coffee, served by friendly staff. Sunny courtyard garden dining area.

③ THE PLATFORM DINER
102 Gillies Street, Kawakawa; tel: 09 404 1110; $
Located in Kawakawa's historic railway station with sheltered platform dining, this established café serves simple home-made fare.

④ CAFÉ OVER THE BAY
Upstairs at The Mall, Marsden Road, Paihia; tel: 09 402 8147; $–$$
Enjoy a healthy menu and lots of vegetarian options from Paihia's Café over the Bay. As the name implies, the views are impressive.

⑤ ALFRESCOS
6 Marsden Road, Paihia; tel: 09 402 6797; $–$$
This quaint, boutique-style café is perfect for a quick coffee or light breakfast or lunch, and has ample outdoor seating with bay views. Dinner menu features fresh seafood, steak and NZ lamb rump.

Above from left:
Northland beach; carved Maori mask, Waitangi National Reserve; digging for shellfish on Northland's west coast; fun on Te Paki sand dunes.

On the Water
The essence of the Bay of Islands cannot be experienced without getting out onto the water. Sports fishing is legendary here; famous American game-fisherman Zane Grey was based at Otehei Bay in 1926 and dubbed it 'Anglers' Paradise'. Charter a yacht, board an historic creamboat tour or sail on a traditional tall ship to cruise around this paradise of 144 beautiful green islands hemmed with biscuit-coloured sands and sheltered anchorages. The more adventurous can climb aboard a powerboat for a thrillingly fast excursion to Piercy Island, zipping through the Hole in the Rock.

Russell, once known as 'the hell hole of the Pacific' and famous for its unruly population of whalers and runaways, is now a quiet town with a distinctly Victorian atmosphere. Walk along the waterfront and seek out **Pompallier House** (South End, The Strand; tel: 09 403 9015; www.pompallier.co.nz; daily 10am–5pm; charge), a Catholic mission house dating to 1841, making it the oldest survivor of its type in the country. The gardens are particularly attractive, and have fine views of the Bay of Islands.

Also make time to visit the **Russell Museum** (2 York Street; tel: 09 403 7701; www.russellmuseum.org.nz; daily 10am–4pm; charge), which documents the development of the town from its early days as a Maori village to the present day. Highlights of the col-

lection include a model of Captain Cook's ship *Endeavour*. Other activities in Russell include hiking up Flagstaff Hill, where Maori warrior Hone Heke and his men felled the British flagpole four times.

Take a break from your sightseeing at one of the many fine eateries lining the waterfront. The **Duke of Marlborough**, see ⑪⑥, is a good choice for food and is also an option if you want to stay the night in Russell.

Haruru Falls

At this point, return to Paihia, as there are a couple of sights nearby well worth visiting. The first is **Haruru Falls ❽**, once the location of New Zealand's first river port. To reach the falls drive 3km (2 miles) down Puketona Road, or, if you're feeling adventurous, explore this waterway by kayak with Coastal Kayakers (Te Karuwha Parade, Ti Bay, Waitangi; tel: 09 402 8105; www.coastalkayakers.co.nz).

Waitangi Treaty House

After viewing the falls, retrace your route and then follow the signs to the **Waitangi National Reserve ❾** (tel: 09 402 7437; www.waitangi.net.nz; daily, summer 9am–7pm, winter 9am–5pm; charge). Allow at least an hour to stroll the grounds and view the **Whare Runanga** (Maori meeting house), which depicts the ancestors of many Maori tribes in its intricate carvings, *waka* (Maori war canoe) and the **Waitangi Treaty House**, where New Zealand's founding document was signed in 1840. Have lunch at the

---

Food and Drink 🍴

⑥ DUKE OF MARLBOROUGH

35 The Strand, Russell; tel: 09 403 7829; www.theduke.co.nz; $$–$$$
The menu at the restaurant in this smart waterfront boutique hotel has French foundations with strong New Zealand influences. Oysters, mussels and other seafood are brought straight from the sea to the table.

⑦ POSH NOSH

3 Homestead Road, Kerikeri; tel: 09 407 7213; closed Sun; $
Serves Mediterranean cuisine throughout the week with a stress on Spanish dishes on Friday. Try their divine gazpacho made using Kerikeri tomatoes. The breakfast menu is wide-ranging European fare and comes with freshly roasted coffee.

contemporary Waikokopu Café, located in the Treaty House grounds, or return in the evening for a recommended cultural production performed by local Maori (tel: 09 402 5990; www.culturenorth.co.nz; charge).

TOWARDS CAPE REINGA

At this point you can either return to Auckland via SH1 on the route already travelled, return via the West Coast's SH12, or travel north for another 223km (140 miles) to **Cape Reinga**. The round trip to Cape Reinga can be completed as a day's drive from Paihia but it's worth taking longer. Alternatively, a number of operators, including Fullers (Maritime Building, Paihia Wharf; tel: 09 402 7421; www.fboi.co.nz), run coach and four-wheel-drive tours from Paihia. Most drive one way via the beach highway of Ninety Mile Beach *(see p.40)* and return by road.

Kerikeri

For those driving themselves north, breakfast is best enjoyed in the vibrant township of **Kerikeri** ⑩, a haven for the gourmet traveller with locally produced wine, olives and avocados, cheese, ice cream and chocolate; try **Posh Nosh**, see ⑪⑦, for refreshment.

Before you leave town visit the historic **Kemp House** (246 Kerikeri Road, Kerikeri Basin; tel: 09 407 9236; daily, summer 10am–5pm, winter 10am–4pm; charge), New Zealand's oldest-standing European building, erected in 1822 by the Reverend Gare

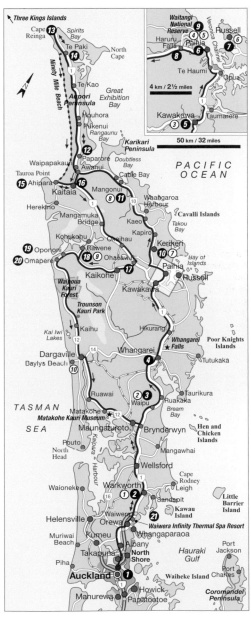

Maori Tradition

According to Maori traditions, the spirits of the departed leap from an 800-year-old pohutukawa tree on the windswept Cape Reinga to begin the voyage back to their final resting place in the ancestral homeland of Hawaiki.

Butler as a mission house. Also look out for the adjacent **Stone Store** (times as above), built in 1832 to house food for the mission.

Mangonui, Awanui and Paparore

Continue north on SH10 through the fishing village of **Mangonui** ⑪, home to New Zealand's best fish-and-chip shop, see ⑪⑧, and on to **Awanui**, rejoining SH1. At Awanui, the **Ancient Kauri Kingdom** (229 SH1, Awanui; tel: 09 406 7172; www.ancientkauri.co.nz; daily 9am–5pm; free), where 30,000–50,000-year-old swamp kauri logs are crafted into a range of furniture and housewares, is worth a look.

Nearby, in **Paparore** ⑫, the **Gumdiggers Park** (171 Heath Road; tel: 09 406 7166; www.gumdiggerspark.co.nz; daily 9am–5pm; charge) offers an insight into the old gum-digging days – when settlers dug for kauri gum, used to make varnish – at its 100-year-old gumfield.

Cape Reinga

Rejoin the northbound SH1 to **Cape Reinga** ⑬. This is a place of great spiritual significance to Maori people, who believe it is 'the place of the leaping', where the souls of the dead gather before they enter the next world *(see left)*. Weather permitting, the **Three Kings Islands**, named by Abel Tasman in 1643, will be visible on the horizon, while the spectacular Cape Maria Van Diemen dominates the west. To the east the long curve of Spirits Bay leads the eye to the North Cape.

THE WEST COAST

Ninety Mile Beach

The icing on the cake of a trip to the Cape involves driving one way along the magnificent sandy highway of **Ninety Mile Beach**, entering or exiting on **Te Paki Stream** ⑭. This is only possible, however, if you are in a non-hire vehicle, as hired cars are not insured on the beach. (If you are in a hire car, simply head south instead on SH1.) The vast Te Paki Dunes at the start of the stream can be reached by road, so consider hiring a sand toboggan onsite to slide down them. Then rejoin SH1 or continue south following the beach's unbroken arch of white sand to **Ahipara** ⑮, at the southern tip.

BACK TO AUCKLAND

To return to Paihia at this point, travel via **Kaitaia** ⑯ and **Kawakawa** on SH1. To return to Auckland from Paihia via the West Coast, turn off SH1 onto

---

Food and Drink 🍴

⑧ MANGONUI FISH AND CHIP SHOP
Beach Road, Mangonui; tel: 09 406 0478; $
Overhangs the Mangonui Harbour and serves fresh, locally caught fish. Succulent bluenose, served with lemon, is the speciality.

⑨ BOATSHED CAFÉ
8 Clendon Esplanade, Rawene; tel: 09 405 7728; $
Situated in a renovated shed on stilts overhanging the harbour, this café does fresh New Zealand fare. From the terrace watch the mist rising from mangroves as water laps beneath your seat.

⑩ FUNKY FISH CAFÉ
34 Seaview Road, Baylys Beach; tel: 09 439 8883; $
A classic Kiwi café with an eclectic mix of tables and chairs in a courtyard garden setting surrounded by sculpture. Seafood is their speciality – the Pacific oysters, garlic prawns and seafood chowder are very good, as is the Northland beef.

SH12 at **Ohaeawai** ⓱. For your first glimpse of the Hokianga Harbour, take the turn-off to **Rawene** ⓲, a picturesque harbourside town on a peninsula. Noteworthy buildings here include **Clendon House** (8 Clendon Esplanade; tel: 09 405 7874; summer Mon–Sat 10am–4pm, winter Mon–Tue 10am–4pm; charge), an 1860s building that was home to James Reddy Clendon, an early trader and member of the first Legislative Council from 1844. Displays in the house give insight into early colonial life.

A good stopping point here is the **Boatshed Café**, see ⓨⓩ, where you can relax and watch the vehicular ferry that transports locals and visitors across to **Kohukohu**. Jump aboard, if you have the time, to explore this once thriving timber town, stamped with early 1900s architecture and featuring NZ's oldest stone bridge.

Opononi

Back on SH12, a 19km (12-mile) drive leads to **Opononi** ⓳, the largest town of the Hokianga, and one-time home of Opo, a young, friendly bottlenose dolphin that adopted the town and played with children in the summer of 1955–6. Morning, afternoon and evening harbour cruises are run daily by Crossings Hokianga (29 SH12, Opononi; tel: 09 405 8207; www.crossings hokianga.com), as are sport fishing and sand tobogganing on the vast dunes at the harbour's entrance. To see local kiwi, book a twilight tour with Footprints Waipoua (29 SH12 Opononi; tel: 09 405 8207; www.footprintswai poua.com; daily; charge).

Omapere and Waipoua Forest

The small town of **Omapere** ⓴, a rest stop on the hill, provides a lasting and dramatic vista of the Hokianga Harbour before you enter the **Waipoua Forest** on SH12. The forest is home to the massive kauri tree and an ideal place to wander in the type of dense vegetation that once cloaked New Zealand. There are several walks to enjoy here, the most popular being the five-minute stroll to see the 2,000-year-old Tane Mahuta, the largest kauri of all.

Kai Iwi Lakes and Baylys Beach

Heading south on SH12, other popular attractions include the **Kai Iwi Lakes** and the pounding shores of **Baylys Beach**, a good stop for refreshment at the **Funky Fish Café**, see ⓨ⓾, before you reach the flats of **Dargaville** and **Ruawai**, lush with kumara (sweet potato) crops.

Be sure to stop at Matakohe to visit the **Matakohe Kauri Museum** (tel: 09 431 7417; www.kauri-museum. com; daily 9am–5pm; charge) and lose yourself for a while in bygone days of kauri-felling, gum-digging and hardy pioneers, before rejoining SH1 to Auckland.

Waiwera Thermal Resort

Consider stopping en route at the **Waiwera Infinity Thermal Spa Resort** ㉑ (21 Main Road, Waiwera; tel: 09 427 8800; www.waiwera.co.nz; Sun–Thur 9am–9pm, Fri–Sat 9am–10pm; charge), where you can relax in the waters of its hot thermal pools before returning to the bustle of the city.

Above: sleepy cat at Kemp House; the Stone Store.

4

COROMANDEL PENINSULA

This two-day driving tour leads from the old gold-mining township of Coromandel, across the ranges to Mercury Bay's magnificent Cathedral Cove, then south to the resort area of Pauanui and Tairua.

Firth of Thames

The Firth of Thames shelters an abundance of birdlife, and provides some of New Zealand's best driving, winding through tiny beachside settlements, interspersed with cliffs gripped by ages-old red-blossoming pohutu-kawa. Along the route, take time to wander through Rapaura Water Gardens; stop in at Tararu's exotic Tropical Butterfly and Orchid Garden; and enjoy an ice cream on the beach.

DISTANCE 452km (281 miles)

TIME Two days

START Auckland

END Auckland or Tauranga

POINTS TO NOTE

You will need a car for this tour; for details of car-hire firms, *see p.111.* Take care as you approach the Kopu Bridge, which spans the Waihou River. It is a long one-lane bridge controlled by traffic lights, so make sure you wait until the lights are green. We recommend a mining tour in Thames, so take sensible footwear with closed toes with you. Aim to arrive at Hot Water Beach *(see p.45)* for low tide, if you can.

Food and Drink

① SOLA CAFÉ

720 Pollen Street, Thames; tel: 07 868 8781; $

In the heart of the Grahamstown area of Thames (to the north of the centre), this vegetarian café serves generous portions, and has a wheat- and gluten-free menu. While you indulge in nutritious fare such as lay-ered eggplant-and-polenta lasagne, you can check out the work of local artisans decorating the café walls.

The scenic Coromandel region is one of New Zealand's most ruggedly beautiful, with waterfalls, secluded hot springs, huge expanses of windswept beach festooned with driftwood, and old gold mines. In the 19th century, the peninsula was exploited for kauri timber, kauri gum (used in varnishes) and gold. Stands of forest were axed, but some remain, providing a home for rare species of frog and native birds, hundreds of kingfishers and sea-bird colonies (the latter can be found on offshore islands). Semiprecious stones such as carnelian, agate, chalcedony and jasper are washed down from the hills into creeks to mingle with the pebbles on the western beaches.

Auckland to Thames

Thames, the gateway to the Coromandel Peninsula, is a straightforward 90-minute drive from **Auckland ①**. Start on Queen Street and drive up to Karangahape Road; turn left, then veer right before Grafton Bridge, following the signs to SH1. Follow SH1 south for about 20km (12½ miles) and shortly after Bombay take the turn-off for SH2, signposted to Tauranga. Follow the highway another 50km (31 miles) before you turn east on to

SH25, signposted to Thames. The road heads out across the low-lying former swamplands of the Hauraki Plains. Over 1,000km (620 miles) of drains and canals have turned this land into productive dairy pasture, though it is still prone to occasional flooding. Cross the Kopu Bridge *(see grey box, left)*, which spans the Waihou River, and you will reach a T-junction at the base of the Coromandel Range. Turn left and drive 5km (3 miles), following the signs to Thames.

THAMES

Nowadays, **Thames ❷** (pop. 7,000) is predominantly a service town for the outlying rural communities, but in the second half of the 19th century, it had the largest population in New Zealand, with around 18,000 inhabitants and well over 100 hotels – due to its goldmines.

Make your first stop the **Tourist Information Centre** – the teal-green building on the right as you enter the town (206 Pollen Street; tel: 07 868 7284; www.thames-info.co.nz; Mon–Fri 8.30am–5pm, Sat–Sun 9am–4pm). Here, you can pick up brochures and information on activities in the region.

Drive down Pollen Street, the town's main thoroughfare, for glimpses of its heyday. Some of the old buildings of the mining era remain, notably the restored (but shut down) **Brian Boru Hotel** on the corner of Richmond and Pollen streets. The **Sola Café**, see ⓵①, is also on Pollen Street, if you need refreshment.

Mining Town

To continue the tour, follow Pollen Street north and turn right back on SH25, then quickly right again for the **Goldmine Experience** (corner of

Above from far left: kayaking around Cathedral Cove; coastal cliffs; sunbather looking out to sea; kiwi protection area.

Coromandel Forest Park
Behind Thames is the Coromandel Forest Park, with 50km (31 miles) of well-maintained hiking tracks to explore.

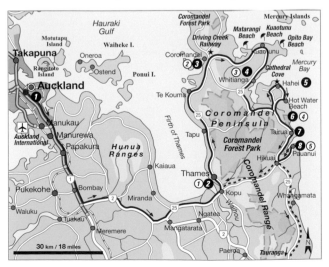

SH25 and Moanataiari Road; tel: 07 868 8514; www.goldmine-experience.co.nz; daily 10am–4pm; charge).

The original site of the 1868 Gold Crown claim now features a photographic exhibition of Thames. The well-informed hosts will take you on a tour of an old mine shaft; the tour, which takes at least 40 minutes, can be muddy during the wetter months, so go prepared with closed-toe footwear. For those who dislike being in confined dark spaces, there are alternative activities here, including gold-panning.

COROMANDEL TOWNSHIP

Continue north on SH25, travelling along the waterline on a route lined with pohutukawa trees (red-blossoming New Zealand Christmas trees) that grow so thickly that the telephone lines have to leave the bank and journey across the water instead, to **Coromandel ❸**. Take a walk around the town, which has an arty atmosphere, to admire its Victorian buildings and relics from the gold-mining and timber industries. For a bite to eat, visit **Pepper Tree**, see 🍴②, on Kapanga Road, in the centre.

Head north up Buffalo Road to soak up local history. First, try your hand at gold-panning and admire the waterwheel at the **Coromandel Stamper Battery** (410 Buffalo Road; tel: 07 866 7933; Sat–Thur 10am–5pm; charge). Return to the main road, then turn right onto Driving Creek Road for the **Driving Creek Railway** (380 Driving Creek Road, Coromandel; tel: 07 866 8703; www.drivingcreekrailway.co.nz;

daily 10am–5pm; charge), a 30-year-old project still evolving under the direction of Barry Brickell, one of the country's most respected potters. A narrow-gauge 15-inch track, with tunnels, spirals and a double-decker viaduct, zigzags uphill past sculptures to the 'Eyeful Tower', a wooden terminus with gorgeous views of the Firth of Thames.

WHITIANGA

After your exploration of Coromandel township, resume your drive, crossing the Coromandel Range on SH25. En route to Whitianga, visit the beautiful East Coast beaches of Matarangi, Kuaotunu and Opito Bay.

Whitianga ❹ is the main hub for marine-based activities departing for the **Te Whanganui A Hei Marine Reserve**, which stretches from Cooks Bluff and Motukoruro Island through to Mahurangi Island. Charter boats such as *Escapade* (tel: 07 867 1488; www.islandcruise.co.nz; charge) offer sightseeing cruises and fishing trips, including game fishing opportunities. Pit stops here include **Wild Hogs**, see 🍴③, on the beach, a five-minute walk from the centre of town.

HAHEI

Make time to visit the village of **Hahei ❺**, 16km (10 miles) south. Here, you can rent a kayak for a guided trip to the stunning **Cathedral Cove**, where a gigantic arched cavern penetrates the headland, with Cathedral Cove Kayaking (88 Hahei Beach Road; tel:

07 866 3877; www.seakayaktours.co.nz; daily; charge), or hop aboard the *Hahei Explorer* (6 Wigmore Crescent, Hahei; tel: 07 866 3910; www.haheiexplorer. co.nz; daily 10am and 2pm; charge). Cathedral Cove can also be reached on foot, on a track that leads down from a lookout point above Hahei.

HOT WATER BEACH

To soak in your own freshly dug pool at **Hot Water Beach** ❻, drive south 10km (6 miles) and turn off, following the signs to Hot Water Beach. Aim to arrive around low tide (your accommodation hosts or Visitor Information Centre will be able to advise you on tide times). Hire a spade for $5 from **Hot Waves Café**, see ⑪④, or borrow one from your accommodation, and stroll north along the beach. A rocky outcrop marks where you can dig holes in the sand. Wallow in the hot-spring waters until the tide begins to turn.

Note that it is not safe to swim at Hot Water Beach, owing to strong currents.

TAIRUA AND PAUANUI

Further south on SH25 is the town/ resort of **Tairua** ❼. The very best views of its harbour and white beach can be had from the top of Mount Paku – Maori legend has it that if you climb to the peak of the mountain you'll return within seven years; the outstanding views may entice you to do this anyway.

The neighbouring community of **Pauanui** ❽ is a popular playground

for wealthy Aucklanders and a great place to relax. Popular local activities include swimming, surfing, fishing, diving, bush walks and golf. **Miha Restaurant**, see ⑪⑤, is only a short stroll from the beach.

BACK TO AUCKLAND

From here, you can return to your base in Auckland via SH25A, which travels through the Coromandel Forest Park to Kopu, where you can retrace your steps to Auckland. Alternatively, you can link this tour to the next one *(see p.46)* and continue on to Tauranga. To do so, drive 34km (21 miles) south on SH25 to the summer beach resort of **Whangamata**, after which it is an easy 100km (62-mile) journey through the gold-mining township of Waihi and on to SH2 to Tauranga.

Whangamata

In Whangamata, beach life reigns, and surfers rule; fishing is immensely popular, and even swimming with dolphins is not an infrequent occurrence. With two good golf courses, mountain biking in the forest and walking trails including the Wharekirauponga, Wentworth Valley and Luck at Last Mine tracks, there are lots of landbased activities to enjoy too.

Food and Drink 🍴

② PEPPER TREE
31 Kapanga Road, Coromandel Township; tel: 07 866 8211; $$
Serves light, fresh New Zealand cuisine at breakfast, lunch and dinner. Space for indoor and outdoor dining.

③ WILD HOGS
9 The Esplanade, Whitianga; tel: 07 866 4828; $–$$
Right on the beach with magnificent views, Wild Hogs serves delicious wood-fired pizzas and a range of Pacific Rim cuisine. Open for lunch and dinner.

④ HOT WAVES CAFÉ
8 Pye Place, Hot Water Beach; tel: 07 866 3887; $–$$
Hot Waves serves delicious home-made food in an ambient mud-brick building. Tables spill into a large native bush garden.

⑤ MIHA RESTAURANT
Mount Avenue, Pauanui Beach; tel: 07 864 8088; $$$
Pacific Rim flavours blended with a modern European twist.

TAURANGA DISTRICT

*This driving tour of the Tauranga District in the Bay of Plenty can begin
from Rotorua, travelling through the kiwifruit-growing area of Te Puke
to Mount Maunganui, or in reverse in conjunction with tour 4 (see p.42).*

Kiwi-Farming
The fertile soils and
warm climate of the
Bay of Plenty nurture
the vines that
produce 80 percent
of the country's
kiwifruit behind
tall windbreaks.

Below: Mount
Maunganui and
Tauranga Harbour.

DISTANCE 166km (103 miles)
TIME A full day
START/END Rotorua
POINTS TO NOTE
A car is needed for this journey; for car-hire firms, *see p.111*. Allow about 90 minutes for the direct return journey from Rotorua to Tauranga. Bring a swimming costume, if you want to bathe at the spa at the end of the tour.

The Tauranga District is an easy day trip
from Rotorua, 86km (53 miles) along an
attractive northbound route. It is part of
the Bay of Plenty, an area that the Maori
travelled vast distances to reach in a
series of migrations over several hundred
years. Since then, the relaxed settlements
along this coastline have continued to
draw visitors from far and wide.

TOWARDS OKERE FALLS

In **Rotorua ❶**, start at the **i-SITE
Visitor Information Centre** on Fenton
Street. Turn left and follow SH30 out of
town, travelling past Te Ngae and the
airport, and continuing straight on
SH33 to Okawa Bay and Lake Rotoiti.
Make **Okere Falls ❷**, at the head of
Lake Rotoiti, your first stop. Take the
sharp left turn just past the Okere Falls
shop and follow the signs to a small car
park. This is the start point of an easy
10-minute walk along the Kaituna River
to a lookout point. If you're feeling

Food and Drink 🍴
① KIWI 360 CAFÉ
SH2, Te Puke; tel: 07 573 6340; $
Enjoy lunch on a covered balcony overlooking the vines. The excellent menu includes seafood, salads, posh pizzas and freshly baked cakes, including own-recipe kiwifruit muffin.

adventurous you can whitewater raft its 7m (23ft) falls, the highest commercially rafted waterfall in the world, with Raftabout (Okere Falls Bridge, SH33; tel: 07 343 9500; www.raftabout.co.nz; daily 9am, 12.30pm and 3.30pm).

TE PUKE

Continuing for about 25km (15½ miles) by car from Okere Falls, watch for signs to **Spring Loaded Fun Park** ❸ (316 SH33, Paengaroa; tel: 07 533 1515; www.springloadedfunpark.co.nz; daily 9am–5pm; charge). Here, daredevils can hop aboard a jet-boat ride for a spin up the Kaituna River, learn to four-wheel-drive on an adventure track, or take a scenic helicopter flight.

Kiwi 360

Shortly after Spring Loaded Fun Park, the road meets SH2. Make a left turn here towards the fertile soils of **Te Puke**, New Zealand's major kiwi-fruit-growing area. Just past the turn-off to Whakatane is a sculpture of the giant kiwi fruit that marks **Kiwi 360** ❹ (35 Young Road, Te Puke; tel: 07 573 6340; www.kiwifruitcountry.co.nz; daily 9am–5pm, tours 9.30am–4pm; charge, tours only); this working kiwi-fruit farm offers informative rides through the orchards aboard a cart train. The café here, see ⑪①, is a popular choice for lunch.

MOUNT MAUNGANUI

A roundabout 16km (10 miles) beyond Te Puke signals the approach of Tauranga and **Mount Maunganui** ❺.

Do not veer left on SH2, but continue on what becomes Maunganui Road. Follow it for about 4km (2½ miles) to reach what locals dub 'The Mount'. This refers to the town's namesake, Maunganui, a conical rocky headland that rises to a height of 232m (761ft) above sea level and was one of the largest early Maori settlements in New Zealand.

The well-signposted **i-SITE Visitor Centre** (Salisbury Avenue; tel: 07 575 5099; www.bayofplentynz.com) can provide maps to hikes on the mountain.

Follow Salisbury Avenue round past the sheltered **Pilot Bay** to the base of The Mount, park near the Domain

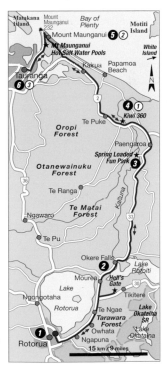

Above from far left: disused wharf pillars in Tauranga Harbour; the view from Mount Maunganui over Mount Maunganui and Papamoa Beaches; the unmistakable giant kiwifruit, marking Kiwi 360.

Up the Mountain
The extinct volcanic cone of Mount Maunganui rises above a safe, sheltered inner-harbour beach. The walkway that leads to the mountain's summit is dotted with seats offering amazing harbour, ocean and city views.

Above from left:
shady trail leading up
Mount Maunganui;
gondola ride over
Rotorua; having a
crazy time Zorbing.

White Island
In the southern Bay
of Plenty is the lunar
landscape of White
Island, where jagged
red ridges rise around
yellow and copper
fumeroles, discharging
gas so pressurised it
roars like a squadron
of B52 bombers.
Despite the formidable
terrain, the island has
incredible allure,
mainly since this is the
only place in the world
where you can see an
active marine volcano
at such close
proximity. For further
information, contact
White Island Tours
(15 The Strand East,
Whakatane; tel: 07
308 9588; www.white
island.co.nz).

campgrounds, then follow signs to the
start of the tracks. Depending on how
energetic you feel, you can either take
the Summit Road Track to the top of
the mountain, or enjoy a stroll on the
circular track around the base.

Have a picnic on the beach at Pilot
Bay or head to Marine Parade to tackle
the surf on the sweeping white sands
of Mount Maunganui Beach. Inexpen-
sive food can be purchased from any of
the tearooms and cafés that line Maunganui Road; **Sand Rock Café**, see ①②,
is our recommendation.

TAURANGA

After lunch make your way to **Tauranga
❻**, driving back along Maunganui
Road and cutting a sharp right at the
roundabout to head along SH29
(Hewletts Road) and over the harbour
bridge. As you come off the bridge,
follow the signs left at the roundabout
to the city centre and park your car on
The Strand near the railway station.
Stroll to the north end of **Herries Park**
and cross the road to see the ceremonial canoe, *Te Awanui*, on display.

A path at the base of the hill takes
you through the pleasant **Robbins
Park** and **Rose Garden** to the **Mon-
mouth Military Redoubt**. British
troops were stationed here during
unrest in the 1860s, and their earth-
works and guns survive as reminders of
the bloody conflict between Maori and
Pakeha in days gone by.

Back on The Strand, a short walk
brings you to the main shopping
precinct and Devonport Road, where
you can enjoy afternoon tea at a local
café such as **The Med**, see ①③, before
retracing your steps to Rotorua.

Pools and Spas
On the way back, stop at the **Mount
Maunganui Hot Salt Water Pools** (9
Adams Avenue; tel: 07 575 0868; www.
tcal.co.nz; Mon–Sat 6am–10pm, Sun
8am–10pm; charge) for a refreshing
swim, or a communal mud spa overlooking the thermal reserve at **Hell's
Gate** (tel: 07 345 3151; www.hellsgate.
co.nz; daily 8.30am–8.30pm; charge),
in Tikitere.

To get to the pools, turn off SH33
5km (3 miles) after Mourea on to
SH30 and travel 4km (2½ miles),
parking right outside the complex.
Take a stroll around the thermal park,
where highlights include an accessible
mud volcano and the beautiful **Kakahi
Falls**, the largest hot waterfall in the
southern hemisphere, before suc-
cumbing to the glorious mud spa. Here
you can cake yourself with detoxifying
mud, then soak in a hot thermal pool.
Go private at the adjoining (more
expensive) Wai Ora Spa.

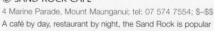
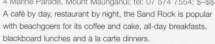

Food and Drink 🍴

② SAND ROCK CAFÉ
4 Marine Parade, Mount Maunganui; tel: 07 574 7554; $–$$
A café by day, restaurant by night, the Sand Rock is popular
with beachgoers for its coffee and cake, all-day breakfasts,
blackboard lunches and à la carte dinners.

③ THE MED
62 Devonport Road, Tauranga; tel: 07 577 0487; $
Tasty all-day breakfasts, deli-style salads, pastries and sandwiches, and a range of hot dishes on a blackboard menu.

ROTORUA

Set amid crater lakes, Rotorua offers stunning scenery in an active volcanic wonderland of spouting geysers, bubbling mud pools, fumaroles and natural thermal springs. This driving tour covers its highlights.

Rotorua, as the locals proudly boast, is the only place in New Zealand where you can tell exactly where you are with your eyes closed. They are referring, of course, to the distinctive aroma of sulphur that permeates the town, courtesy of its boiling mud pools and hot springs. To visit Rotorua with your eyes shut would be a travesty, however, because it is an area of rich cultural and scenic beauty. Block your nose and head out boldly; you will soon become accustomed to the smell.

The town (pop. 64,500) was a popular tourist destination in the 1800s, when visitors came to marvel at the naturally formed Pink and White Terraces *(see p.53)*. Today, it is one of the jewels of New Zealand tourism, a place of thermal wonders, lush forests, green pastures and crystal-clear lakes abounding with fighting trout. No fewer than ten lakes are now the playground of anglers, campers, swimmers, water-skiers, yachtsmen and hunters.

Rotorua is also a major centre for Maori culture – one third of the city's population is Maori. Marae (tribal meeting-places) dot the area.

GONDOLA RIDE

Start from the **Rotorua i-SITE Visitor Centre** (1167 Fenton Street; tel: 07 348

DISTANCE 33km (20 miles)
TIME At least a full day
START/END Rotorua
POINTS TO NOTE

A car is needed for this journey; for car-hire firms, *see p.111.* Bring a swimming costume if you want to bathe at the Polynesian Spa.

5179; www.rotoruanz.com; daily 8am–5.30pm). From the centre, make a left turn onto Arawa Street, then turn right on to Ranolf Street (the start of SH5). This drive takes you past **Kuirau Park** on your left, a 25-hectare (62-acre) public reserve (free) where you can pull over to see several steaming fumeroles.

Continue on, following Ranolf Street as it morphs into Lake Road. At the end of Lake Road at the traffic lights, turn right onto Fairy Springs Road. Travel about 4.5km (3 miles), then turn left into the car park at **Skyline Skyrides Gondola ❶** (tel: 07 347 0027; www.skylineskyrides.co.nz; daily 9am–late; charge). Within minutes of buying a ticket you will be whisked sharply up the 900m (2,953ft) slopes of Mount Ngongotaha for glorious views of the region that you will soon be exploring; there's a **café** here, see ⑪① *(p.50)*, if you would like refreshment.

Thrills and Spills

Rotorua is the place to dive out of your comfort zone into any number of crazy thrills. A good place to begin is at the Agrodome in Ngongotaha (Western Road, Ngongotaha; tel: 07 357 1050; www.agrodome.co.nz; daily 8.30am–5pm; charge), 6km (4 miles) from the city centre. Climb into a Zorb, a big, fat, clear-plastic ball, and roll full tilt downhill, protected from serious harm by an air cushion. If that's not wacky enough, you can kit up in a flying suit, goggles and gloves, and levitate spreadeagled in mid-air above a 150kmh (93mph) blast of jet stream rushing from a 900-hp twin-turbo DC3 aircraft propeller.

Above from left:
cycling is a great way to tour Rotorua; steamy ground and hot springs; rafting Kaituna Falls.

On the return journey, ride back down on the gondola or take the luge, a three-wheel cart, on the exciting 1km (³/₄-mile) long downhill track.

RAINBOW SPRINGS

A further 100m/yds along Fairy Springs Road is **Rainbow Springs Kiwi Wildlife Park & Rainbow Springs Kiwi Encounter ❷** (tel: 07 347 9301; www.rainbowsprings.co.nz; daily, summer 8am–11pm, winter 8am–10pm; charge), showcasing more than 150 species of native New Zealand fauna set among freshwater springs and pools filled with rainbow and brown trout. There's a nice café here – **The Springs Café**, see ⑪②. Directly opposite on the other side of Fairy Springs Road is the **New Zealand Caterpillar Experience** (tel: 07 347 3206; www.caterpillarexperience.co.nz; daily 8.30am–5pm; charge), a museum dedicated to an intriguing display of vintage Caterpillar earth-moving machinery.

AROUND LAKE ROTORUA

Return to your car and follow SH5 back towards town, turning off on to Lake Road. Stop at the lakefront parking area near the jetty, where every day at 12.30pm the *Lakeland Queen* (tel: 0800 572 784; www.lakelandqueen.com; charge), a 22m (72ft) paddle steamer, takes passengers around **Lake Rotorua** from the **Lakeland Queen Launch Jetty ❸** on a lunchtime cruise. (Note that breakfast and dinner cruises are also available.)

While dining you will be regaled with the love story of Hinemoa and Tutanekai, a Maori legend similar to *Romeo and Juliet*, but with a happier ending. (If you miss the boat, you can eat at the **Lakeside Café**, see ⑪③.)

Ohinemutu

There's plenty to see around the lake, so after lunch take a stroll northwest of the café along the narrow driveway that heads past the **Rotorua Yacht Club**

Food and Drink 🍴

① TERRACES CAFÉ
Fairy Springs Road; tel: 07 347 0027; $
A broad menu ranges from the all-day breakfast to freshly made sandwiches and cakes, fish and chips to pizzas and sushi.

② THE SPRINGS CAFÉ
Fairy Springs Road; tel: 07 350 04440; $
This place does a filling 'Big Breakfast' and is popular for its steak ciabatta and Cajun chicken salad. You can dine amid the café's own vegetable gardens, with many tables providing waterfall views.

③ LAKESIDE CAFÉ AND CRAFTS SHOP
Memorial Drive; tel: 07 349 2626; $–$$
If you miss the boat, or choose not to sail, 50m/yds to your left (facing the lake) is the Lakeside Café and Crafts Shop, where you can have lunch and browse through a selection of works by local artisans.

④ THE THAI RESTAURANT
1147 Tutanekai Street; tel: 07 348 6677; $
Authentic country-style Thai cuisine with robust flavours. A lively night market is held nearby on Thursday evenings.

⑤ THE INDIAN STAR
1118 Tutanekai Street; tel: 07 343 6222; $–$$
Fully licensed or BYO wine, The Indian Star offers a wide ranging feast of Indian cuisine. This is where locals come to order their takeouts.

⑥ CICCIO ITALIAN CAFÉ
1262 Fenton Street; tel: 07 348 1828; $$–$$$
Fashionable café serving light and tasty pasta dishes and pizza.

and along the waterfront to **St Faith's Church** and **Ohinemutu** ❹. This tiny lakefront village was the main settlement here when Europeans arrived in the 1800s. Today it's renowned for its idyllic little church, built in 1885, with its beautiful stained-glass window, an etched window depicting a Maori Christ figure who looks as though he is walking on the waters of Lake Rotorua, and a bust of Queen Victoria. The church was presented to the Maori people of Rotorua in appreciation of their loyalty to the Crown and is an impressive expression of how the Maori adopted Christianity into their traditional culture.

Tutanekai Street

Leaving the lakefront, walk to **Tutanekai Street**. The north end of Tutanekai is Rotorua's café hotspot; dining options include **The Thai Restaurant**, **The Indian Star** and **Ciccio Italian Café**, see ⑪④–⑥. Further south you will find a wide variety of shops, including a vast number of souvenir stores.

Museum of Art and History

Now head east on Arawa Street and Queens Drive, past the Convention Centre and into the Government Gardens. Within its grounds is the **Rotorua Museum of Art and History** ❺ (Queen's Drive; tel: 07 349 4350; www.rotoruamuseum.co.nz; summer daily 9am–8pm; charge). The 1908 Tudor-style building showcases art exhibitions and displays of slightly sinister-looking apparatus used for

hydrotherapy more than a century ago. Permanent exhibitions tell the story of the local Te Arawa people and the devastating eruption of Mount Tarawera in 1886.

WHAKAREWAREWA

It's now time to practise pronouncing the name of your next destination, **Whakarewarewa** (far-car-rear-wah-rear-wah), the closest thermal area to the city. To reach its two major

Raised Graves
Another of Ohine-mutu's curious features are its raised graves, laid out in this way because of the thermal activity below ground.

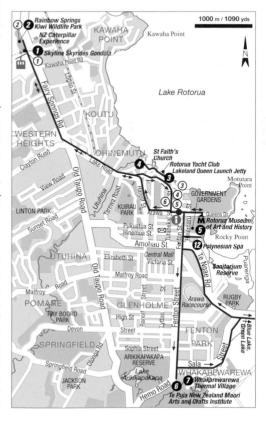

Above from left:
mud, glorious mud;
spectacular views of
the Tarawera Crater;
a restorative mud
treatment face pack.

attractions, head to the **Rotorua i-
SITE Visitor Centre** (1167 Fenton
Street) and travel south for 3km (2
miles), following the road as it veers
right into Hemo Road. On the left is
Te Puia, home of the famous Pohutu
Geyser and the **New Zealand Maori
Arts and Crafts Institute** ❻ (SH30;
tel: 07 348 9047; www.nzmaori.co.nz;
daily 8am–6pm; charge), where you
can watch Maori carvers and flax
weavers at work. Guided tours leave on
the hour, every hour until 5pm and
take in the works of the arts institute
as well as bubbling mud pools, boiling

hot springs, and the Pohutu Geyser,
which erupts up to 30m (98ft) high.

Allow at least 2–3 hours to explore
this area and the adjacent **Whakarewarewa Thermal Village** ❼ (17 Tryon
Street; tel: 07 349 3463; www.whakare
warewa.com; daily 8.30am–5pm;
charge). You can take a guided tour and
meet the Tuhourangi/Ngati Wahiao
people who live among the geothermal
activity and make use of the energy
garnered from hot springs and steam
vents for cooking purposes, as well as
the natural mineral waters for communal bathing. The area's geysers can
be viewed from safe platforms.

BLUE AND GREEN LAKES

From Whakarewarewa, it's a scenic
20-minute drive to the Blue and
Green Lakes. Head back up Fenton
Street towards town and turn right
into Sala Street; follow the street out
to Te Ngae Road (SH30) and then
turn off on Tarawera Road, the first
main road to your right. Approximately 10km (6 miles) from the city,
along the forest-fringed Tarawera
Road, you suddenly drop down to
opalescent **Lake Tikitapu**, otherwise
known as the **Blue Lake** ❽.

Weather permitting, this is a great
place for a swim; alternatively, you can
hike around its shoreline (1.5 hours) or
hire a canoe or pedal boat from the Blue
Lake Holiday Park across the road.

Continuing on, the road rises to a
crest, from which you can see Lake Tikitapu and the larger **Lake Rotokakahi**,
or **Green Lake** ❾, resting side by side.

Food and Drink 🍴

⑦ BURIED VILLAGE CAFÉ
Tarawera Road; tel: 07 362 8287; $
The café within the Buried Village offers home-cooked fare such
as cakes, biscuits, slices, freshly filled rolls and hot savouries.

The waters of the Green Lake are *tapu* (sacred) to local Maori, and are not open for watersports.

PINK AND WHITE TERRACES

The road continues along an historic tourist route opened in the 19th century to the former **Pink and White Terraces**, once known here as the eighth wonder of the world. The naturally formed silica terraces on the shores of Lake Rotomahana were like a giant staircase, with a fan-shaped edge spilling across almost 300m/yds of lakefront. But nature proved unkind to its own wonders, and on 10 June 1886 a massive volcanic eruption of Mount Tarawera obliterated the terraces and buried two Maori villages beneath layers of ash and mud.

Te Wairoa

A memorial to the tragedy is located just a few minutes' drive past the Green Lake – the **Buried Village ⑩** excavation of Te Wairoa (1180 Tarawera Road; tel: 07 362 8287; www. buriedvillage.co.nz; summer daily 9am–5pm; charge). Parking is available in front of the Buried Village souvenir shop and **café**, see ⑪⑦.

A marked walk takes you through the village excavations and sites, including its Maori *whare* (house), a flour mill, blacksmith's shop, a store and a hotel. Take in the village's eerie atmosphere in the shade of poplar and sycamore trees, a legacy of the early European settlers – and keep an eye out for the *whare* in which a Maori elder, who had foretold the tragedy, was trapped for four days before being rescued alive.

Depending on time and energy levels, you can either make your way past an animal enclosure back to the entrance to the Buried Village, or take the longer, but highly recommended, bush track that crosses Te Wairoa stream and leads steeply down through dense native bush to a waterfall and rapids. Continue on this route and you'll arrive back at the souvenir shops and café.

LAKE TARAWERA

From the Buried Village, Tarawera Road continues to **Lake Tarawera ⑪**, where a lookout point en route provides good views of the hulk of Mount Tarawera across the lake. Take the first left downhill to **Tarawera Landing**, located on a quiet pumice-fringed bay with a small jetty. Lake cruises, guided trout fishing charters, and self-drive boats, kayaks and pedal boats can be hired from The Landing Café.

SPA DELIGHTS

There's no better way to end a day in Rotorua than a soak in thermally heated water. Retrace the route back to Fenton Street and turn right into Hinemoa Street to the lakeside **Polynesian Spa ⑫** (Lake End, Hinemoa Street; tel: 07 348 1328; www.polynesianspa.co.nz; daily 8am–11pm; charge). Here you can enjoy a relaxing dip in restorative geothermal waters and perhaps treat yourself to a therapeutic massage.

Tamaki Maori Village
Time permitting, top off this busy day with a pre-booked Maori cultural show at the Tamaki Maori Village (SH5; tel: 07 349 2999; www.maori culture.co.nz; daily 6.30pm; charge). You'll be collected from your accommodation and taken on a 20-minute bus journey to a replica village in an atmospheric forest. Local guides introduce Maori culture, myths and legends, song and dance, and perform the *Chronicles of Uitara*, a story spanning several generations of a warrior tribe. Tickets include a multi-course evening meal. At the close of ceremonies, you can end the evening with a *hongi* – a traditional pressing of noses to signify friendship.

TAUPO

This driving tour is an easy day trip from Rotorua, heading south to Orakei Korako, then on to Huka Falls and Lake Taupo, New Zealand's largest lake. Stay another day and drive the volcanic loop around the mountainous Tongariro National Park, possibly en route to Wellington.

DISTANCE 96km (59 miles), excluding Tongariro National Park; 343km (213 miles) including the park
TIME One to two days
START Rotorua
END Rotorua or Wellington
POINTS TO NOTE
You will need a car for this tour; for details of car-hire firms, see p.111. Book in advance for any therapeutic treatments you might want at Taupo Hot Springs (see p.57).

Above from left: still morning on Lake Taupo; jet boat on the Waikato River.

Below: Huka Falls.

New Zealand's largest lake, Lake Taupo, is fed by sparkling ice-melt from the mountains of the Tongariro National Park. It was formed by volcanic activity – an eruption so large that it was recorded by Chinese and Roman writers. The region's extraordinary landscape and unique range of cultural experiences make it a 'must-see' on any New Zealand itinerary.

The township of Taupo is situated on the shores of Lake Taupo, about 90km (56 miles) south of Rotorua. From the **i-SITE Visitor Centre** (1167 Fenton Street) at **Rotorua ❶**, follow the road south past **Whakarewarewa** on to SH5.

THERMAL WONDERLAND

For a day tour, you will need to choose one option from the following three thermal parks listed; if you plan to stay overnight in Taupo there will be time to fit in at least two options.

Waimangu Volcanic Valley

About 20km (12½ miles) south of Rotorua on SH5 you will pass the turn-off to **Waimangu Volcanic Valley ❷** (587 Waimangu Road; tel: 07 366 6137; www.waimangu.com; daily 8.30am–5pm; charge), a hotbed of thermal activity unearthed by the

1886 eruption of Mount Tarawera. Attractions here include the volcanic area around Waimangu Cauldron, the Inferno Crater, Ruamoko's Throat, typified by craters, volcanic lakes and hot springs, and a boat cruise to see the steaming cliffs of Lake Rotomahana. A walk through the valley, returning by shuttle bus (excluding the boat ride), takes about one to two hours.

Wai-o-Tapu

Back on to SH5 and 10km (6 miles) further south you will pass the turn-off for the **Wai-o-Tapu Thermal Wonderland ❸** (Loop Road; tel: 07 366 6333; www.geyserland.co.nz; daily 8.30am–5pm; charge). This sight is famous for the **Lady Knox Geyser**, which (with a little human assistance – eco-friendly soap is used to release the surface tension) blows its top at 10.15am each day, and the boiling Champagne Pool, which flows over green silicate terraces. Allow at least an hour to explore.

Lake Ohakuri

Closer to Taupo (22km/13¹⁄₂ miles past the turn-off to Atiamuri) look for the signposts leading to **Orakei Korako ❹** (494 Orakei Korako Road; tel: 07 378 3131; www.orakeikorako. co.nz; daily 8am–4.30pm; charge) on the shores of **Lake Ohakuri**. A boat waits to ferry travellers to a pristine geothermal field surrounded by unique silica terraces. Encompassing 35 active geysers, plopping mud pools and fizzing hot springs, this park also features an extremely rare geothermal cave. Allow an hour to explore.

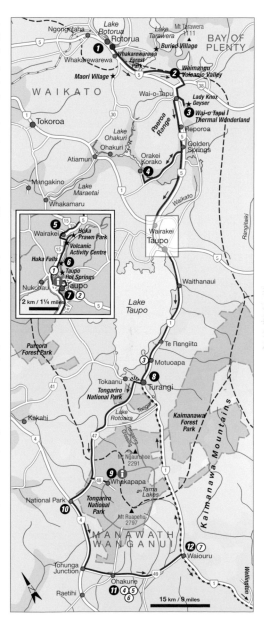

Taupo Watersports

Lake Taupo regularly plays host to international watersports events and is popular with residents and visitors alike for sailing, kayaking, windsurfing and numerous other sports and activities.

Below: serious business at the Huka Prawn Park.

WAIRAKEI PARK

Continue driving: only 2km (1¼ miles) before **Wairakei ❺**, SH5 joins with SH1. Just past Wairakei, on your left, look for the turn-off to the **Volcanic Activity Centre** (Wairakei Park; tel: 07 374 8375; www.volcanoes.co.nz; Mon–Fri 9am–5pm, Sat–Sun 10am–4pm; charge), which has informative displays on the region's geography.

Huka Prawn Park

This section of the Waikato River includes the world's only geothermal prawn farm, the **Huka Prawn Park** (Wairakei Park, Taupo; tel: 07 374 8474; www.hukaprawnpark.co.nz; daily 9.30am–3.30pm; charge), where you can feast on juicy tropical prawns while enjoying views of the river as it begins its 425km (264-mile) journey to the sea.

Honey Hive

Also in the park is the **Honey Hive** (Wairakei Park; tel: 07 374 8553; www. honeyhivetaupo.com; daily 9am–5pm;

free), the country's largest honey centre, selling honey-scented soaps, lotions and wine. There's also honey-tasting, a picnic area and a ride for children.

Jet-Boat Ride

Leaving here, follow the signs from the car park for a thrilling spin on the Waikato River with Huka Jet boat rides (Wairakei Park; tel: 07 374 8572; www.hukajet.co.nz; daily 10am–4.30pm, departures every half-hour). This adrenaline-pumping ride is guaranteed to leave you breathless.

HUKA FALLS

The most stunning feature in this area is the thundering **Huka Falls ❻**. To reach them, turn left and follow the signs 2km (1¼ miles) to the Huka Falls car park. A short walk takes you to views of the falls, where up to 270 cubic metres (9,535 cubic ft) of water are tumultuously pushed through a long, narrow gorge before plunging into a deep pool. There are several good walks in the area, including the four-hour return journey along the river to the Aratiatia Rapids.

Pit stops on the Huka Falls Road include the **Huka Vineyard Restaurant**, see ①.

TAUPO

From here it's a short car ride through to **Taupo ❼**. Make a stop at the signposted lookout on the left just heading into town; it provides panoramic views of the lake and mountains of the Tongariro National Park. This vast

expanse may seem serene, but don't be fooled; over the past 27,000 years this crater has erupted 28 times. Hot springs and spas are testimony to the fact that this region has not yet run out of steam.

Follow SH1 from here into Taupo township. The Taupo **i-SITE Visitor Centre** (Tongariro Street, Taupo; tel: 07 376 0027; www.laketauponz.com; daily 8.30am–5pm) is on your right as you enter the town. If you want to pick up brochures from here, continue past it to the lakefront, turn right into the lakeside car park, then walk back.

Lake Taupo

Now follow the road down to the wharf and marina, where various cruises depart across **Lake Taupo** throughout the day. Highly recommended is a trip on the *Ernest Kemp*, a replica 1920s steamer, which leaves daily at 10.30am and 2pm, with an extra sailing at 5pm during summer (tel: 07 378 3444; charge).

Alternatively, hop aboard a catamaran tour with Chris Jolly (14 Rauhoto Street, Taupo Boat Harbour; tel: 0800 252 628; www.chrisjolly.co.nz; daily 10.30am and 2pm; charge) and cruise around Acacia Bay and Rangatira Point, bound for Whakaipo Bay, where contemporary Maori rock carvings can be seen on a cliff face. These were commissioned by the Queen Elizabeth Arts Council in 1980 and created by artists of the local Tuwharetoa tribe.

If you would like refreshment at this point, walk north up Tongariro Street and take the third right, Horomatangi Street; **Salute Deli Café**, see ①②, is at no. 47.

Bungy-Jumping and Hot Springs

Those with energy to burn may want to delay lunch and instead bungy-jump over the **Waikato River** with **Taupo Bungy** (202 Spa Road, Taupo; tel: 07 377 1135; www.taupobungy.co.nz; daily 8.30am–5pm; charge). Also located on site is Taupo's newest attraction, the **Taupo Cliff Hanger**, an extreme swing ride that reaches speeds of up to 70kmh (44mph). Just beyond the jump site is a parking area. It's an easy walk from the lower car park down to the river's edge, where you can paddle in a natural hot spring that mixes with cold river water.

Alternatively, soak in thermal pools ranging from 37 to 41°C (99–106°F), at **Taupo Hot Springs** (Napier-Taupo Highway; tel: 07 377 6502; www.taupohotsprings.com; daily 7.30am–9.30pm; charge), followed by a therapeutic massage. Booking is essential.

Food and Drink 🍴

① HUKA VINEYARD RESTAURANT
56 Huka Falls Road, Taupo; tel: 07 377 2326; $$–$$$
Taupo's only winery restaurant serves up mouthwatering cuisine in an exquisite setting of landscaped gardens and pinot noir vines. Enjoy one of the chef's signature dishes, such as filet mignon, while seated on the expansive patio with panoramic views of Mount Tauhara. Cellar door-style wine tastings are available at the bar.

② SALUTE DELI CAFÉ
47 Horomatangi Street, Taupo; tel: 07 377 4478; $
If you are hanging out for a super-fresh salad or grilled sandwich, this is the place to visit.

Above from far left: Tongariro's barren volcanic landscape, which served as Mordor in the *Lord of the Rings* movies, is punctuated by vividly coloured lakes and lava formations; the mountains in winter.

Lake Taupo
Lake Taupo last erupted 1,800 years ago; its average depth is 110m (360ft); its length is 46km (25 nautical miles); its width is 33km (18 nautical miles); and its total area is 616 sq km (238 sq miles). During winter the lake averages 11°C (52°F) and in summer 18°C (64°F).

The lake is known for its fabulous trout fishing, but in New Zealand it is illegal to buy or sell trout, so if you wish to dine on this delicacy you must catch your own. Enquire at the i-SITE Visitor Centre, where staff will match you up with an experienced local skipper or guide. Skilled fly-fisherfolk will enjoy the wilderness experience of Taupo's wealth of local rivers, but bear in mind that river fishing operates purely on a catch-and-release basis.

Above from left:
skiing at Whakapapa;
natural steam bath;
mountain fun.

Ski Country
In winter, the Whaka-
papa Ski Field, 8km
(5 miles) from Whaka-
papa Village, teems
with snowboarders
and skiers of all
abilities. Huge, snow-
filled basins with steep
chutes, drop-offs and
powder stashes
provide an ample
playground for all; a
variety of lessons is
available. Turoa Ski
Field, on the other
side of the mountain,
has a wide-open bowl
that faces southwest
and offers good
conditions in October
and November.

If you are doing this tour as a day
tour, retrace your steps at this point
to take you back to Rotorua. If you
want to continue the tour, stay
overnight in Taupo *(see p.115)*, then
follow on as described below.

VOLCANIC LOOP

The first stop on the second day of this
tour is Tongariro National Park, which
offers blue and emerald lakes, waterfalls,
rocky plateaux, twisted thickets of native
bush, huge open landscapes and snowy
slopes, and can easily be explored from
Taupo or en route to Wellington.

Turangi
Head out of Taupo on SH1 and drive
through Motuoapa, where the **Licorice
Café**, see ⑪③, provides a good breakfast stop, and on to **Turangi ❽**, a village
on the banks of the Tongariro River.

Turangi is the place to rediscover the
thrill of angling or to take a ride aboard
a whitewater raft with **Tongariro River
Rafting** (tel: 0800 101 024; www.
trr.co.nz; departures daily: summer 9am
and 2pm, winter noon; charge).

Tongariro National Park
Leaving Turangi on SH47, make a stop
at the lookout on the right-hand side
before continuing the ascent through
dense forest into **Tongariro National
Park**. Beneath Mount Tongariro, with
its red craters, is **Lake Rotoaira** and the
Opotaka Historic Reserve (free).

After passing the reserve, you'll see
brown, windswept plains of toitoi,
manuka and flax, then the charred
cinder cone of **Mount Ngauruhoe**,
which last erupted in 1975. Man-
gatepopo Road provides access to the
Tongariro Crossing, New Zealand's
best one-day hike *(see box, below left)*.

The majestic snowy crown of **Mount
Ruapehu** dominates the route (SH48)
to **Whakapapa Village ❾**, a small ski
village with a range of accommodation
and cafés. The Visitor Centre provides
information on local hikes, including
the Mount Ruapehu summit walk,
Taranaki Falls and Tama Lakes.

At this point, if the budget allows,
take a scenic flight with Mountain Air
(corner of SH47/48; tel: 07 892 2812;
www.mountainair.co.nz; daily 8am–
5pm). Alternatively, continue on SH47
to the township of **National Park, ❿**
a home from home for snow junkies in
the winter ski season, with a climbing
wall, equipment hire and bars and cafés,
at the junction of SH47 and SH4.

Tongariro Crossing

The 17km (10½-mile) Tongariro Crossing, New Zealand's best one-
day hike, passes the steep, charred sides of Ngauruhoe, the
mineral-stained walls and active fumeroles of Tongariro's Red
Crater, and the vivid Emerald Lakes, contrasting sharply with
the burnt earth hues of the surrounding lunar-like landscape. Further on is the gleaming Blue Lake, also known as Te Rangihiroa's
Mirror, after the son of a
chief who explored the region
in AD 1750. The views are
spectacular. The hike finishes
on SH46, and transport to and
from the track can be organised at all local hotels.

Ohakune

Follow SH4 south to Tohunga Junction, then turn off onto SH49 to **Ohakune** ⓫, a fast-growing après-ski hub. Ohakune offers easy access to the Turoa ski slopes up the picturesque mountain road dense with mountain beech forest, dwarf shrubs, and alpine flowers and shrubs. Lunch spots here include the **Alpine Restaurant**, **Mountain Kebabs** and **Utopia Café**, see ⑪④–⑥.

Waiouru

From Ohakune, SH49 continues on to rejoin SH1 at **Waiouru** ⓬, home to the NZ Army's largest training camp and the **Army Memorial Museum** (SH1, Waiouru; tel: 06 387 6911; www.army museum.co.nz; daily 9am–4.30pm;

charge), where a sensitively curated collection of army memorabilia captivates military enthusiasts and civilians alike. The museum café, **Reload**, see ⑪⑦, is a good place for a break.

END OF TOUR

From here, you can choose to return to Taupo via SH1, travelling through the dry, desolate landscape of the Rangipo 'desert', before retracing your route back to Rotorua; alternatively, continue south towards Wellington. The 370km (236-mile) journey on SH1 takes around five hours from Taupo, or 261km (162 miles) and four hours from Waiouru, and travels through Taihape, Bulls, Levin, and then down the Kapiti Coast to Wellington.

Tangiwai Tragedy

Proof of the region's volatile geology can be seen at the Tangiwai rail disaster memorial, on SH49 between Ohakune and Waiouru. Here, in 1953, a lahar flooded the Whangaehu River, destroying the Tangiwai Railway Bridge and killing 153 people. Fortunately, when Mount Ruapehu's Crater Lake burst its banks again, in March 2007, an alarm system provided a warning, before a torrent of mud and debris poured through the river gorge.

Food and Drink 🍴

③ LICORICE CAFÉ
57 SH1, Motuoapa, Turangi; tel: 07 386 5551; $
Licorice Café is where those in the know go. The menu changes daily but always features a total of six gluten-free and vegetarian meals, plus a range of other home-cooked Kiwi fare, including the ever-popular wood-smoked salmon salad.

④ ALPINE RESTAURANT
Corner of Clyde and Miro streets, Ohakune; tel: 06 385 9183; $$
This smart restaurant does European-style cuisine. The atmosphere is warm and welcoming.

⑤ MOUNTAIN KEBABS
29 Clyde Street, Ohakune; tel: 0800 532 227; $
The name says it all – freshly made, reasonably priced kebabs are found here.

⑥ UTOPIA CAFÉ
47 Clyde Street, Ohakune; tel: 06 385 9120; $–$$
Great coffee, all-day breakfasts and delicious café fare served throughout the day until 4–5pm. Open fire in winter.

⑦ RELOAD CAFÉ
SH1, Waiouru; tel: 06 387 6911; $
This popular café, housed in Waiouru's Army Memorial Museum, serves breakfast from early in the morning, and hearty gourmet burgers, stuffed with the likes of chicken, brie and cranberry, for lunch.

WELLINGTON

Vibrant Wellington, the seat of government and the unofficial cultural centre of the country, has a cosmopolitan buzz. This full-day walking tour explores its many highlights.

DISTANCE 4km (2½ miles)
TIME A full day
START Museum of New Zealand
END Courtenay Place
POINTS TO NOTE

Enjoy a leisurely start to this tour, as the Museum of New Zealand only opens at 10am.

What's in a Name?
The earliest name for Wellington, from Maori legend, is Te Upoko o te Ika a Maui. This means 'the head of Maui's fish'. Caught and pulled to the surface by Polynesian navigator Maui, the fish became the North Island. Evidence of early Maori settlement and cultivation can be found at sites all across the Wellington Peninsula.

Wellington has an assurance and an international flair that comes with being the country's artistic and cultural heart as well as its capital city. With a regional population of about 440,000, including about 200,000 in the city itself, Wellington is considerably smaller than its northern rival, Auckland, which it replaced as capital in 1865.

Recent Development

Although a quiet, unassuming place until the late 20th century, in the last couple of decades New Zealand's capital has blossomed into a vibrant, urban destination with a lively nightlife. The city's charm derives partly from its quirky topography, with wooden turn-of-the-20th-century houses clinging to steep hillsides bristling with native bush and clumps of arum lilies. Zigzag streets spill downwards to the heart of

the city, the harbour and the affluent promenade of Oriental Bay. The layout reminds some visitors of San Francisco.

Wellington is nicknamed the 'Windy City', and that's no exaggeration; it's usually breezy, and at times the wind can knock you clean off your feet. In the business district, old higgledy-piggledy Wellington has virtually been replaced by soaring modern buildings – a cause of regret for many who loved the haphazard character of the old layout.

MUSEUM OF NEW ZEALAND

The tour starts at the **Museum of New Zealand – Te Papa Tongarewa ❶** (55 Cable Street; tel: 04 381 7000; www.tepapa.govt.nz; Fri–Wed 10am–6pm, Thur 10am–9pm; free), the city's star attraction. It has a vast collection, incorporating interactive displays, virtual-reality games and special exhibitions (many of which change frequently), so pick up a map in the foyer first to make the most of your time here.

Highlights

The museum's highlights include the permanent exhibition of Maori myths and legends of creation, a simulated earthquake, displays of bones of the

extinct giant moa (a flightless bird, hunted into extinction in the 16th century) and a swing-bridge walk through a section of re-created native bush.

CITY CENTRE

To see more of the city, head north out of Te Papa, following the waterline towards the city's commercial centre. Watch out for in-line skaters as you make your way past the rowing clubs by **Frank Kitts Park**. Situated across the road is the city's vast **Civic Square ❷**, home to the **Michael Fowler Centre** (a concert and conference hall), the Edwardian-style **Town Hall** and the **Wellington City Library**, a gorgeous plaster curve of a building, decorated with metal palms. Tucked away between these civic buildings is the Art Deco **City Gallery** (tel: 04 801 3021; www.citygallery.org.nz; daily 10am–5pm; free), known for its

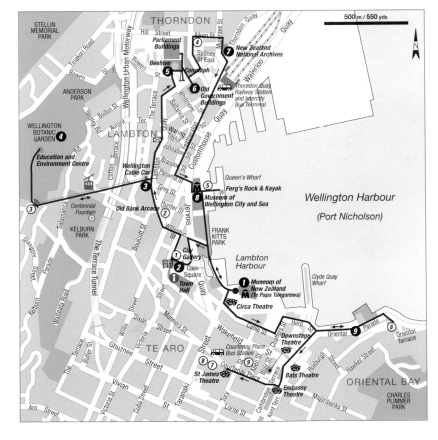

Above from left: sign for Museum of New Zealand – Te Papa Tongarewa *(see p.60)*; cable car to Upland Road and the Botanic Garden; the Beehive.

contemporary art exhibitions (and home to the **Nikau Café**, see ⑪①), and the **Wellington i-SITE Visitor Centre** (tel: 04 802 4860; www.wellingtonnz.com; daily 8.30am–5pm).

Lambton Quay

Head west, leaving the square via the archway next to the library. Cross Victoria Street and walk one more block north to Willeston Street. Turn left. After one block Willeston merges with **Lambton Quay**, the heart of the city's commercial and retail area. Banks, accountancy and law firms vie with shop owners here and on **The Terrace**, a block behind, for some of the country's most expensive retail space.

There was once a quay on this site, before an earthquake in 1855 pushed a rocky ledge permanently into place around the harbour's edge. Land was then steadily reclaimed to create more space for the city. Browse the shops and take a stroll through the stunning Victorian **Old Bank Arcade**, on the corner of Hunter Street and Lambton Quay. Combine boutique shopping with a refreshment break at **Caffe Astoria**, see ⑪②.

New Zealand Designers
Wellington's shopping scene is second to none. Designer names to look out for include Karen Walker, Zambesi *(catwalk show illustrated above)* and local Wellingtonians Mandatory, Starfish, Voon and Andrea Moore.

Wellington Cable Car

About 150m/yds up Lambton Quay you will see the sign for the **Wellington Cable Car** ❸ (Lambton Quay; tel: 0800 801 700; www.wellington cablecar.co.nz; Mon–Fri 7am–10pm, Sat 8.30am–10pm, Sun 9am–10pm; charge). Cars leave every ten minutes and take you effortlessly up a steep incline, under the motorway and over

Kelburn Park to Upland Road for splendid views. There is an excellent viewing point at the upper terminus.

Adjacent to this is the **Wellington Cable Car Museum** (1 Upland Road; tel: 04 475 3578; www.cablecarmus eum.co.nz; daily 9.30am–5pm; free), which tells the story of New Zealand's last operational cable-car system. A good choice for lunch is the **No1 Bistro & Bar**, see ⑪③.

BOTANIC GARDEN

If the weather is good, take a stroll after lunch around the adjacent **Wellington Botanic Garden** ❹ (daily dawn–dusk; free), 25 hectares (62 acres) of protected native forest, conifers, specialised plant collections and floral displays. It is classified as a Garden of National Significance by the Royal New Zealand Institute of Horticulture and is an Historic Places Trust Heritage Area.

Wander off the main paths to appreciate the gardens fully, but ultimately aim for the **Education and Environment Centre** (Mon–Fri 9am–4pm, Sat–Sun 10am–4pm), where you can learn about New Zealand's flora.

Afterwards, return to the cable car for the ride back to Lambton Quay.

THE BEEHIVE

After disembarking the cable car, turn left back on to Lambton Quay and walk to the end where it meets Bowen Street. Cross over and you are at the circular **Beehive** ❺, the seat of political power in New Zealand. Designed by the

British architect Sir Basil Spence and constructed between 1969 and 1980, it houses the executive wing of Parliament, including the office of the Prime Minister. Walk past the **Cenotaph**, through the gates, and follow the sweeping drive up to the Beehive and the adjacent **Parliament Buildings**, dating to 1922.

Make your way to the **Visitor Centre** (tel: 04 471 9503; Mon–Fri 10am–4pm, Sat 10am–3pm, Sun 11am–3pm; free) in the foyer for an informative 1-hour guided tour that runs on the hour. The tour provides insight into how the building was 'earthquake-proofed' during its last renovation.

Old Government Buildings

Also of interest here are the **Old Government Buildings ⑥**, set opposite the Cenotaph on Lambton Quay. Claimed to be the largest wooden building in the southern hemisphere, it was erected in 1876 using over 9,290 sq m (100,000 sq ft) of timber.

If you're thirsty, head 50m/yds up Molesworth Street, which runs in front of the Parliament grounds, to the **Backbencher** pub and café, see ⑪④.

NATIONAL ARCHIVES

From the Backbencher, walk down Aiken Street to Mulgrave Street. At the **National Archives ⑦** (10 Mulgrave Street; tel: 04 499 5595; www.archives. govt.nz; Mon–Fri 9am–5pm; free), you can view New Zealand's national records, including the nation's founding document, the Treaty of Waitangi.

QUEEN'S WHARF AREA

From the National Archives building, head back into town along Mulgrave Street; walk past Thorndon Quay Railway Station, then continue straight along Featherston Street for seven blocks to the intersection with Panama Street. Turn left onto Panama and cross **Customhouse Quay** to Queen's Wharf. Here, the New Zealand Academy of Fine Arts (tel: 04 499 8807; www.nzafa. com; daily 10am–5pm; free) exhibits a range of arts and crafts.

Nearby, housed in the 1892 Bond Store Building, is the **Museum of Wellington City and Sea ⑧** (tel: 04 472 8904; www.museumofwellington. co.nz; daily 10am–5pm; free), which

Food and Drink 🍴

① NIKAU CAFÉ
City Gallery Building, Civic Square; tel: 04 801 4168; Mon–Sat; $
Contemporary café with floor-to-ceiling windows and a sheltered, sun-drenched courtyard. Coffee, wine, snacks and light lunches are served here.

② CAFFE ASTORIA
159 Lambton Quay; tel: 04 473 8500; $$
Reminiscent of a Viennese coffee house, this café is a favourite haunt of the corporate crowd. Come here for snacks, light lunches and dinner and, of course, the coffee.

③ NO1 BISTRO & BAR
1 Upland Road; tel: 04 475 3578; $–$$
Accessed by cable car, this is a top choice for lunch as all tables provide 180-degree views over the city. Light lunches, a snack menu, cakes and coffee, and good cocktails.

④ BACKBENCHER
34 Molesworth Street; tel: 04 472 3065; www.backbencher. co.nz; $$
Everything, including the menu, at this pub has a political theme, and the walls are decorated with cartoons and caricatures of local political figures.

Above from left:
St James Theatre;
Martinborough
Wine Centre.

Katherine Mansfield
One of the city's most
famous daughters,
Kathleen Mansfield
Beauchamp, was born
in 1888 to a middle-
class colonial family.
She was partly
schooled in England
and left New Zealand
permanently for there
at the age of 18 with
the support of £100
a year from her father.
In England, she moved
in bohemian literary
circles that included
such writers as Virginia
Woolf and D.H.
Lawrence. She was
married twice, firstly
to George Brown, then
to literary critic John
Murray. Under the
pen-name Katherine
Mansfield, she wrote
collections of short
stories, notably
Prelude, Bliss and *The
Garden Party*. She
died of tuberculosis in
1923. To find out
more, visit the restored
two-storey family
home in which she
was born, the
Katherine Mansfield
Birthplace (25 Tinakori
Road; tel: 04 473
7268; www.katherine
mansfield.com; Tue–
Sun 10am–4pm;
charge) in the
Wellington district
of Thorndon.

has a captivating collection of maritime memorabilia, covering the city's
seafaring history from early Maori
interaction to the 1900s. Highlights
include a 12-minute show retelling
Maori creation stories. Afterwards,
pop into **Latitude 41**, see ⑪⑤.

ORIENTAL PARADE

If you still have time on your side, walk
back to the Museum of New Zealand,
then carry on around the waterfront following Cable Street to **Oriental Parade**
❾. Here a stroll around the boardwalk
gives great views over the harbour and
bays; note Wellington's prime residen-
tial real estate clinging to the slopes of
Mount Victoria. Call at the **Parade
Café**, see ⑪⑥, for refreshments.

COURTENAY PLACE

Return via Courtenay Place, Wellington's main entertainment precinct. At
the intersection with Kent Terrace is
the grand old **Embassy Theatre**,
venue of the world premiere of the
final cinematic instalment of *The Lord
of the Rings* trilogy. Further up
Courtenay Place on the left is the **St
James Theatre** (77–87 Courtenay
Place; tel: 04 802 4060; www.stjames.
co.nz), which hosts musical acts and
is home to the **Jimmy Café and Bar**,
see ⑪⑦.

Dinner options nearby include
Molly Malones, see ⑪⑧, on the
corner of Courtenay Place and
Taranaki Street, and **Enigma Café**,
see ⑪⑨, at 128 Courtenay Place.

Food and Drink

⑤ LATITUDE 41
19 Jervois Quay, Queen's Wharf; tel: 04 473 8776; $
Serves delicious café fare; Pandoro bread and salads (10 kinds) are its speciality.

⑥ PARADE CAFÉ
148 Oriental Parade; tel: 04 939 3935; $
Popular and welcoming café and restaurant on the seafront promenade, featuring an
open fire in winter and a sunny courtyard in summer. Great food at low prices.

⑦ JIMMY CAFÉ AND BAR
Westpac St James Theatre, Courtenay Place; tel: 04 802 6930; $
Located just inside the entrance to the theatre, this is the perfect place to conclude
the day's sightseeing and plan your evening's entertainment over a coffee.

⑧ MOLLY MALONES
Corner Courtenay Place and Taranaki Street; tel: 04 384 2896; $–$$
An Irish pub/restaurant serving authentic Irish bar snacks with a separate upstairs
dining area dubbed 'The Red Head'. The aged sirloin and pork belly are splendid.

⑨ ENIGMA CAFÉ
128 Courtenay Place; tel: 04 385 2905; $
Locals throng to this funky café/bar for its counter food and alcoholic beverages.

THE WAIRARAPA

This tour takes you out of Wellington, over the Rimutaka Ranges and into the Wairarapa region. Highlights include Martinborough's vineyards, Greytown's colonial architecture and the imposing, rugged coastline.

The scenery of the southern Wairarapa region is ruggedly dramatic: rolling tablelands end abruptly to form high, textured cliffs, the Rimutaka Ranges cast shadows over Lake Wairarapa, and, to the north, the Tararua Ranges tower over fertile plains. At the centre of this is Martinborough, a town that is internationally recognised for its pinot noir.

Wellington to Featherston

Start in **Wellington ❶**, at the railway station on Bunny Street. Turn left on to Waterloo Quay, driving past the Westpac Trust Stadium and following signs to the Wellington/Hutt motorway. This takes you along the western edge of Wellington Harbour. There are several sets of traffic lights to slow your progress through Lower Hutt, Stokes Valley and Upper Hutt. From here SH2 begins its windy climb over the Rimutaka Ranges. Stop at the top for views of the range's bush-clad hills and, beyond, to the plains of the Wairarapa.

FEATHERSTON

A 16km (10-mile) drive brings you to the town of **Featherston ❷**, where you can pick up regional information from the **Featherston Visitor Centre** (tel: 06 308 8051; www.wairarapanz.com; daily 10am–1pm), housed in the Old Court-

> **DISTANCE** 202km (125 miles) return or 346km (214 miles) including the South Coast
> **TIME** At least one day
> **START/END** Wellington
> **POINTS TO NOTE**
> You will need a car for this tour; for details of car-hire firms, see p.111. Martinborough is an 81km (50-mile) drive from Wellington, but the tour takes longer than expected because the road over the Rimutaka Ranges is so winding. To avoid rush-hour congestion, leave very early (around 6.30am) or head off after 9am.

house building on Fitzherbert Street. On the corner of Fitzherbert and Lyon streets is Featherston's main attraction, the **Fell Engine Museum** (tel: 06 308 9379; www.fellmuseum.org.nz; daily 10am–4pm; charge), home to the only Fell locomotive in the world.

POW Memorial

Now continue north on SH2. Just 1km (⅔ mile) past Featherston you will pass a **POW Memorial**; it is on the site of a former World War I army training barracks, which was also used to hold Japanese soldiers captured in the Solomon Islands during World War

Above: signs of historic Greytown.

Drink Driving
The legal limit for drinking when driving is a blood alcohol content of 0.08 percent for those over 20 years old and 0.03 percent for those under 20 years old. There is a low tolerance of over-stepping these limits, so the advice is not to drink and drive at all.

Divine Chocolate

Next door to the Cobblestones Museum is the divine chocolatier, Schoc Chocolates (177 Main Street, Greytown; tel: 06 304 8960; www. chocolatetherapy. com; Mon–Fri 10am–5pm, Sat–Sun 10.30am–5pm), where organic and preservative-free chocolates and truffles are made on site. Deliciously bitter dark chocolate is a speciality, and their signature lime-chilli range is all the rage in these parts.

II. In an attempted break-out from the camp in 1943, some 48 prisoners lost their lives.

GREYTOWN

A further 11km (7-mile) drive brings you to **Greytown ❸**, New Zealand's first planned inland town. Despite its name, it is anything but colourless; its main street is lined with fine examples of early wooden Victorian architecture. Spend time browsing its boutiques, where you can buy anything from an 18th-century chair and Italian earrings to designer clothes and local art. On the main street, the **Main Street Deli**, see ⑪①, is good for coffee or an early lunch; alternatively, if it's the afternoon, try across the road at **Salute**, see ⑪②.

The **Cobblestones Museum** (169 Main Street; tel: 06 304 9687; daily 10am–4pm; charge) provides a fasci-

nating insight into the region's past. Here you can see Greytown's first Methodist church, erected in 1868; a 100-year-old threshing machine; the intact Mangapakeha school (a single-teacher school, opened in 1902), and the Wairarapa's first public hospital, which dates to 1875. The atmospheric old coaching stables and cobbled grounds (1857) make it easy to imagine the clip-clop of hoofs as stage coaches pulled up here with cargoes of new pioneers.

While you're exploring Greytown, look out for the enormous eucalyptus tree outside St Luke's Church, on Main Street. The story goes that Samuel Oates brought the first wheeled vehicle (a wheelbarrow) over the Rimutakas 150 years ago, bearing a cargo of seedlings. Three seedlings 'disappeared' in Greytown, and the results are easy to spot.

MARTINBOROUGH

Any visit to the Wairarapa is incomplete without paying a visit to the township of **Martinborough ❹**, the hub of the wine industry, a short drive from Greytown. Drive south down Greytown's Main Street and veer left off SH2. You will pass several vineyards on the way into Martinborough, as well as the local **Information Centre** (18 Kitchener Street; tel: 06 306 5010; www.wairarapa nz.com; Mon–Fri 9am–5pm, Sat–Sun 10am–4pm).

Wine Tours

With so many vineyards to choose from, the **Martinborough Wine Centre** (6 Kitchener Street; tel: 06 306 9040; www.

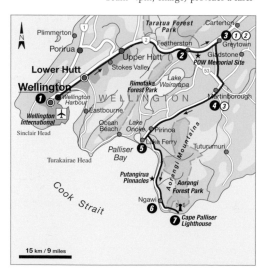

martinboroughwinecentre.co.nz; daily 10am–5pm; free), in the centre of the town, is a good place to start. Here, you can sample a variety of wine from local vineyards and arm yourself with a copy of the Wairarapa and Martinborough wine trail map, ready to explore.

There are around 24 wineries within walking distance of the centre, including **Palliser Estate** (Kitchener Street; tel: 06 306 9019; www.palliser.co.nz; Mon–Fri 10.30am–4pm, Sat–Sun 10.30am–5pm) and **Te Kairanga** (Martins Road; tel: 06 306 9122; www.tkwine.co.nz; daily 10am–5pm).

Hold out for lunch, though, at **Café Bloom**, see ⑪③, on Dry River Road, southeast of Martinborough.

TOWARDS LAKE FERRY

The remainder of the day can be spent sampling wine, perusing local arts and crafts or discovering the scenic south coast. To do this, leave Martinborough on the Lake Ferry Road and head south to **Lake Ferry** ❺, a small settlement with contrasting views over the pounding waves of **Palliser Bay** and tranquil waters of **Lake Onoke**.

Putangirua Pinnacles and Ngawi

Continue on, with the sea on your right, to the **Putangirua Pinnacles** (free), huge, organ pipe-like columns that were formed over the past 120,000 years by heavy rain washing away silt and sand to expose the underlying bedrock.

Further on, in **Ngawi** ❻, a picturesque fishing village at the base of the towering **Aorangi Range**, rows of

brightly painted bulldozers park on the beach. The town does not have a natural harbour, so the bulldozers are used to launch fishing boats from the beach. Keep your eyes open along this coastline for seals *(see right)*.

Cape Palliser Lighthouse

Pick up the same road you were driving on and continue south. High on the edge of a weather-beaten cliff is the **Cape Palliser Lighthouse** ❼, constructed in 1896, and marking the southernmost point of the North Island. Hike the 258 steep steps to the top, from where you can gain magnificent views across the Cook Strait to the snowcapped mountains of Kaikoura.

End of the Tour

On the return journey, if it's getting late, consider spending a night at the elegant colonial-style **Peppers Martinborough Hotel** *(see p.116)*; alternatively, take SH53 to Featherston, where you can pick up SH2 back to Wellington.

Above from far left: colonial architecture; the apple industry is big in this part of the country; keep an eye out for seals in Ngawi, but be sure to maintain the recommended distance of 10m (33ft); Cape Palliser Lighthouse.

Wine makers
The Wairarapa region produces about 3,000 cases of wine per year and is particularly successful with the pinot noir grape. On the wave of Martinborough's wine boom, a flurry of boutique vineyards has opened in the north in Gladstone, East Taratahi, Masterton and Te Puna.

Food and Drink

① MAIN STREET DELI
88 Main Street, Greytown; tel: 06 304 9022; $
Freshly prepared deli-style food and excellent coffee can be enjoyed inside or out, in a pleasant leafy courtyard setting.

② SALUTE
83 Main Street, Greytown; tel: 06 304 9825; $–$$
Unpretentious Salute offers Middle Eastern flavours and fine wines. There's a log fire in winter and shady oaks outside in summer.

③ CAFÉ BLOOM
284 Dry River Road, Martinborough; tel: 06 306 9165; $–$$
Platters, fresh salads and Kiwi favourites, such as grilled salmon fillet, are served on the terraces at Murdoch James Vineyard.

FERRY TO THE SOUTH ISLAND

Cruise across the scenic Cook Strait, keeping your eyes peeled for dolphins, seals and seabirds. Visit the vineyards of Blenheim in the heart of the Marlborough wine country, and either stay overnight there or return to Wellington.

DISTANCE 54km (33 miles), excluding the crossing
TIME At least one day
START Wellington
END Wellington or the South Island (see below)
POINTS TO NOTE

If you do this tour independently (ie not by organised tour), you will need a car; for details of car-hire firms, see p.111. Doing the tour as a self-drive will set you up to start exploring the South Island, possibly by linking up with tour 11. Drive times are as follows: Picton to Blenheim 30 minutes; Blenheim to Kaikoura around 2 hours; Kaikoura to Christchurch 2½ hours. If you stay overnight, there are good options in Picton, Blenheim and Kaikoura (see p.116).

Using **Wellington ❶** as a base, you can make a day trip to Picton in the South Island, visit the wineries of Blenheim or join a mail cruise, and return to Wellington later in the day. The tour can either be done as an organised trip or an independent drive; the information below explains what to expect from both options.

ORGANISED TOURS

The Interislander (tel: 0800 802 802; www.interislander.co.nz; call centre Mon–Fri 8am–8pm, Sat–Sun 8am–6pm) offers this trip – which is somewhat confusingly called the 'Half Day Marlborough Wine Trail', although it is actually a full-day tour. Check-in is at 7.40am for an 8.25am departure, with a scheduled arrival time in Picton of around 11.35am. Another option is the full-day Sounds Delivery Cruise. Check-in is also at 7.40am for an 8.25am departure. Upon arrival in Picton, you board a catamaran for a three-hour cruise, dropping off mail and supplies to resorts and homes inaccessible by road.

Picton and Blenheim

The early arrival leaves plenty of time to explore the waterfront area in

Below: on a whale-watching tour.

Picton ❷, where attractions include the **EcoWorld** aquarium and wildlife centre (Dunbar Wharf; tel: 03 573 6030; www.ecoworldnz.co.nz; charge), the **Edwin Fox Maritime Museum** (Dunbar Wharf; tel: 03 573 6868; www.edwinfoxsociety.com; daily 9am–5pm; charge), documenting the history of the world's ninth-oldest ship, plus shops and cafés, such as **Le Café**, see ⓘ①, on London Quay, close to the Town Wharf.

At 1.30pm the guided half-day Marlborough Wine Trail tour departs from the **Sounds Connection Office** (10 London Quay) bound for the vineyards of **Blenheim ❸**, where there's a chance to taste a selection of wines from four of the region's top vineyards. The Sounds Delivery Cruise also departs at 1.30pm, from the Cougar Line office on the Town Wharf.

The wine-tasting tour concludes at 5.30pm at the Picton terminal, ready for the return journey to Wellington on the MV *Aratere* at 6.05pm (arrives Wellington 9.15pm; meals are available on board). Alternatively, you can elect to remain in Picton for a 10.25pm ferry departure (arrives in Wellington at 1.35am). The latter option provides the opportunity to

enjoy a leisurely evening meal in Picton. The Sounds Delivery Cruise concludes at 4.30pm and provides the same return ferry options.

SELF-DRIVES

If you've rented a car, take it on the ferry with you, or hire a car in Picton. Some rental companies allow you to leave your North Island vehicle in Wellington and pick up a new car in Picton. If you are taking your vehicle across, The Interislander is one of two major companies travelling the Cook Strait between Wellington and Picton; the other is Bluebridge (tel: 0800 844 844; www.bluebridge.co.nz).

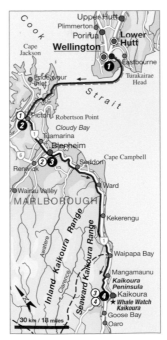

Above from far left: spectacular Kaikoura; Marlborough wine country, at the northern tip of the South Island.

Picton Township
The main attraction of Picton township is soaking up the atmosphere of its buzzing foreshore. Here, kids can sail model yachts in a small pool for 20c a pop, and there's a playground, a merry-go-round, and an 18-hole mini golf course. Relax under a Phoenix palm, watch the coming and going of various sea craft and the tide or, if you are feeling energetic, purchase a picnic and hike out to 'The Snout', a peninsula protruding into the Queen Charlotte Sound (1½ hours return), and spy on dolphins.

Above from left:
whales can be identified by their tails; punting in Christchurch, a city that delights in tradition.

Whale-Spotting
At Kaikoura the chances of spotting a whale are good, thanks to high-tech tracking devices. The sonar 'clicks' from the submerged animals are tracked by a sensitive hydrophone, so the boat can be positioned roughly where the whale will resurface for around 10 minutes, taking breaths before it submerges again. The best part is when the leviathan throws up its flukes and disappears.

Picton and Blenheim
When you arrive in **Picton**, visit the **i-SITE Visitor Centre** (Lagoon Road; tel: 03 520 3113; www.destination marlborough.com) for maps and information, then drive south on SH1 to **Blenheim**, where you can visit wineries producing some of the country's finest sauvignon blanc. Consider eating at **Highfield Estate**, see ⊕②.

Kaikoura
Now continue on SH1 to **Kaikoura ④** on the South Island's East Coast. 'Kaikoura' means 'crayfish food', a name given because of the region's bountiful sea life: sample some at the local restaurants, see ⊕③. The excellent **Hislops Café**, see ⊕④, is a good alternative.

Whale-Watching
A highlight of this part of New Zealand is a tour with **Whale Watch Kaikoura** (Waterfront; tel: 0800 655 121; www.whalewatch.co.nz; tours daily 7.15am, 10am, 12.45pm and 3.30pm; charge). Trips take 2½ hours, and head offshore to view some of the world's biggest mammals in their natural environment. **Whale Watch** is the country's only marine-based whale-watching company, offering close encounters with whales (usually sperm whales in this part of the country) at all times of the year – if you don't see a whale, 80 percent of your tour price will be refunded.

Dolphin Tours
You can frolic with dolphins on a trip out to sea with **Dolphin Encounters** (96 The Esplanade, Kaikoura; tel: 0800 733 365; www.dolphinencounter.co.nz; summer 5.30am, 8.30am, 12.30pm, winter 8.30am, 12.30pm; charge). Allow 3 to 3½ hours for the tour.

Food and Drink 🍴

② HIGHFIELD ESTATE
Brookby Road, Omaka Valley, Blenheim; tel: 03 572 9244; $$
A vineyard restaurant that specialises in matching fresh local produce with wine produced on site. The menu is fluid, depending upon the seasons and subtle changes in flavours of wine.

③ WHITE MORPH
94 Esplanade, Kaikoura; tel: 03 319 5014; $$–$$$
Look no further for the freshest fish, crayfish and Pacific Rim cuisine perfectly matched to a selection of local wines.

④ HISLOPS CAFÉ
33 Beach Road, Kaikoura; tel: 03 319 6971; $
Hislops specialises in wholefoods and organics and has an extensive menu with meat, vegetarian, vegan and gluten-free options. It's a great place to pick up stoneground wholemeal bread (baked daily) for the picnic basket, and enjoy coffee teamed with still-warm muffins.

Whaling
Historic Fyffe House in Kaikoura is the town's oldest surviving building and is located close to where Robert Fyffe established the first shore-based whaling station in 1842. Other stations were subsequently built, and at one stage the industry employed over 100 men. In the 1850s, whale numbers declined, but the industry continued until 1964. In 1978, the Marine Mammal Protection Act was passed, providing protection to all of New Zealand's cetaceans and seals.

DUNEDIN AND THE OTAGO PENINSULA

This combined walk/drive tour explores Dunedin's historic buildings and the Otago Peninsula's wealth of scenery and wildlife attractions, which include colonies of New Zealand Fur Seals, Northern Royal Albatross and Yellow Eyed Penguins.

Dunedin ❶ (population about 125,000, including 20,000 students) is New Zealand's premier university town and is a place of many firsts. It was the site of New Zealand's first university, first electric trams, first cable-car system, and first daily newspaper, the *Otago Daily Times*, which still goes to print every day. When gold was discovered in Otago in 1861, Dunedin fast became the country's financial centre, and an arrival point for miners from around the globe.

Today, its wealth of Edwardian and Victorian buildings are a sight to behold, as is its scenery and wildlife. Extinct volcanic cones shelter the Dunedin Harbour, a cosy haven for visiting container ships and a real abundance of marine life. Dunedin's flora and fauna and the city's close relationship with it, has become its star attraction.

THE OCTAGON

At the heart of Dunedin is **The Octagon ❹**, a small leafy park bordered by historic buildings. Park nearby, then begin this tour at the **Dunedin i-SITE Visitor Centre** (20

DISTANCE 74.5km (46 miles)

TIME At least a full day or split into two days

START/END Dunedin i-SITE Visitor Centre, The Octagon

POINTS TO NOTE

A car is required for the journey out to the Otago Peninsula; for information on car hire firms *see p.111*. There are several fine sandy beaches along the way so remember to pack a bathing costume. Bring sensible walking shoes to explore Penguin Place, Natures Wonders, and the Royal Albatross Centre at Taiaroa Head.

Below: a colourful mural at the Octagon.

Princes Street; tel: 03 474 3300; www.dunedinnz.com; daily 8.30am–5pm), housed in the new Municipal Chambers, and walk anti-clockwise around the Octagon to **St Paul's Anglican Cathedral B** (tel: 03 477 4931), built from stone from 1915-19. Look inside to see its Gothic Revival pillars rising 40 metres to support the only stone-vaulted nave roof in New Zealand.

Continue on to **Nova Cafe** ⑪①, a great place for refreshments. It's right beside the **Dunedin Public Art Gallery C** (30 The Octagon; tel: 03 477 4000; www.dunedin.art.museum; free), the oldest public gallery in New Zealand, and featuring works by Constable, Monet, and Gainsborough, to name but a few.

Dunedin Railway Station
Allow 30 minutes to peruse the gallery, then continue around the Octagon to Lower Stuart Street. Walk three blocks (300 metres) past the old Allied Press newspaper offices and law courts to the **Dunedin Railway Station D** on Anzac Avenue. Designed by George Troup, this vision of Flemish Renaissance style was built between 1904 and 1906. Featuring a 37-metre (121ft) high square tower, covered carriageways, mosaic-tiled floors, original Doulton china and stained glass detailing, it earned Troup a knighthood. Trains to the spectacular Taieri River Gorge depart from here daily *(see margin)*, and on its first floor is the **New Zealand Sports Hall of Fame** (tel: 03 477 7775; wwwnzhalloffame.co.nz; charge). The museum pays tribute to a variety of sports including rugby and has some curious exhibits including the arm guard worn by All Blacks player Colin Meads when he played a test match with a broken arm.

NORTH DUNEDIN

Allow 30 minutes here, then return to your car. From The Octagon drive north up George Street for five blocks, turn right onto Albany Street, then park your car. On foot explore the **Otago Museum E** (tel: 03 477

5052; www.otagomuseum.govt.nz; daily 10am–5pm; free) at number 419 Great King Street. The museum is home to New Zealand's largest fossil, and is a treasure-trove of Maori and Pacific Island artefacts. The **Otago Museum Cafe** ⑪② is a good place to enjoy light refreshments.

University of Otago
Allow 30 minutes to an hour here, then drive east on Albany Street to the Cumberland Street junction. On the left is the campus of the **University of Otago**, and its main clock tower. Turn right onto Cumberland Street and drive past the historic Law Courts, the magnificent 54 metres (180ft) spire of First Church, and statue of Queen Victoria in Queens Gardens.

OTAGO PENINSULA

The return trip out to Taiaroa Head at the tip of Otago Peninsula, can take anything from 90 minutes to a full day; either way, to fully appreciate its magnificent views, it's best to take the 'low road' out and return via the 'high road'.

To get there, turn left at the southern end of Cumberland Street onto Andersons Bay Road, then continue to the Portobello Road junction. Turn left turn onto Portobello Road, which hugs the waterline all the way to Portobello village, at the heart of the peninsula. Stop for a bite to eat here at Portobello's **Penguin Cafe** ⑪③ or **Cafe 1908** ⑪④,

Food and Drink 🍴

① NOVA CAFE
29 The Octagon, Dunedin; tel: 03 479 0808; $–$$
Located next door to the Dunedin Art Gallery overlooking the Octagon, Nova Cafe is well known for its excellent espresso, delicious set breakfasts and freshly prepared cafe fare. Open daily for breakfast from 7.30am (weekends 8am) until late.

② OTAGO MUSEUM CAFE
419 Great King Street, Dunedin; tel: 03 474 7474; $
Brunches and lunches are made fresh to order here, plus you can choose from pre-prepared cabinet food including sandwiches, filled rolls, salads and freshly made bakery items such as muffins, scones, and slices.

③ THE PENGUIN CAFE
1726 Highcliff Road, Portobello; tel: 03 478 1055; $
Housed in an Art Deco building and offering stunning water views, this cafe offers simple well-priced nourishing fare, from bacon butties and poached eggs on toast for breakfast, through to fisherman's pie and ploughman's for lunch. The espresso is excellent, as is the range of home-baked kiwi favourites.

④ CAFE 1908
7 Harrington Point Road, Portobello; tel: 03 478 0801; $$
Fully licensed dining in a turn-of-the-century building which first opened in 1908 as the Wainui tea rooms and later became the local Post Office. The seafood chowder is especially good here, and it is served along with a range of other popular New Zealand fare including lamb shanks, rump steak, and smoked salmon.

Above from far left:
the ornate Dunedin Railway Station; the Otago Museum offers a hands-on experience; a detail on the Otago University building; pull up for a great view overlooking Otago harbour.

City of gardens
Dunedin is well known for its leafy parks and wide open spaces; amongst these is the Town Belt, a 200-hectare (490-acre) long green swathe that separates the city from the suburbs. It's a great place to walk with heavily wooded areas providing a home for native birds like the tui and bellbird, as well as a number of sports fields where visitors are welcome to spectate.

Taieri Gorge Railway
This great all-weather activity offers a return trip through the spectacular Taieri Gorge, northwest of Dunedin, riding in vintage 1920s wooden carriages or modern air-conditioned steel carriages. To book phone 03 477 4449, or visit www.taieri.co.nz.

then head to the **New Zealand Marine Studies Centre and Aquarium ❷** (tel: 03 479 5826; www.marine.ac.nz; 10am–4.30pm charge) on Hatchery Road. Here you can feed hungry pigfish, peek inside shark's eggs, and view rock pools teeming with colourful sea creatures. The aquarium is also the public face of the Marine Science Department of Otago University and a 60-minute guided tour of the facility departs at 10.30am daily.

Otakou Marae
A further 4km (2½ miles) along the coast at **Otakou ❸**, is a Maori marae with a church and a meeting house. The appearance of the building suggests it to be carved, but it in fact it is made of cast concrete. Three 19th century Maori chiefs are buried at its cemetery and the land here is sacred to local Maori.

TAIAROA HEAD

At the tip of the peninsula, is Taiaroa Head, where you can watch magnificent Northern Royal Albatross riding the breeze using their vast three-metre wingspan to soar above the ocean. The **Royal Albatross Centre ❹** (tel: 03 478 0499; www.albatross.org.nz; daily Apr–Nov 9.30am-4.30pm, Dec–Mar 8.30am–8pm; charge) is the only accessible mainland breeding grounds of these birds *(see margin, right)* and is operated by the Department of Conservation (DOC); guided walks to hides overlooking the nesting sites, depart regularly throughout the day.

Fort Taiaroa and Wildlife Attractions
Taiaroa Heads is also the site of **Fort Taiaroa**, where an old Armstrong Disappearing Gun, transported here in 1886 on the perceived threat of an attack by Tsarist Russia, is cleverly hidden beneath the earth. Its 15cm (6-inch) cannon rises to fire, then sinks beneath the earth for reloading.

Beneath the heads is **Pilot Beach**, where fur seals can often be seen. If time permits, hop aboard an eight-wheel all-terrain vehicle at **Natures Wonders ❺** (1265 Hampton Point Road, Taiaroa; tel: 03 478 1150; www.natureswonders.co.nz; Nov–Apr 10am–7.30pm, May–Oct until 4.15pm; charge), and travel across farmland to observe wildlife including spotted cormorants, little blue penguins, yellow-eyed penguins, and New Zealand fur seal pups, all frolicking in rock pools. Leopard seals, elephant seals and orca are also often seen.

BACK TO DUNEDIN CBD

Two must-see attractions are found on the return journey to Dunedin:

Food and Drink

⑤ BALLROOM CAFE
145 Camp Road, Otago Peninsula; tel: 03 476 1616
High tea, light meals and snacks, and other refreshments are served at this cafe, overlooking the gardens of Larnach Castle. Note that entry to the grounds or castle must be paid to dine at this cafe.

Penguin Place, home to hundreds of nesting yellow-eyed penguins, and Larnach Castle, both located on the 'high road'.

At the charming **Penguin Place** ❻ (45 Pakihu Road; tel: 03 478 0286; www.penguinplace.co.nz; daily tours from 10.15am; charge) you can spy upon yellow-eyed penguins from a network of cunningly designed burrows which twist through the dunes along a rugged, sandy beach. Bookings are essential during summer (Dec–Mar).

Larnach Castle

Allow 90 to complete the tour, then retrace your earlier route to Portobello and turn left onto Highcliff Road, the 'high road' back to the city. Along the way visit **Larnach Castle** ❼ (145 Camp Road; tel: 03 476 1616; www.larnachcastle.co.nz; daily

9am–5pm; charge), a 140-year-old baronial manor that is New Zealand's only castle. It took 14 years to build (from 1871) and was the home of the Hon. William J.M. Larnach, financier and later Minister of the Crown. Only the best would do for Larnach and he sourced materials from around the world: these included marble from Italy, tiles from England, slate from Wales and glass from Venice and France. Most of the castle's 43 rooms are open to the public and refreshments can be enjoyed at the **Ballroom Cafe** 🍴⑤.

From Larnach Castle, rejoin Highcliff Road which offers fabulous views of the harbour and city, then turn right onto Greenacres Road. Follow this to MacAndrew Bay, then turn left onto Portobello Road, and retrace the earlier route back to the city centre.

Above from far left: Northern Royal Albatross on Taiaroa Head, Otago Peninsula; pay a visit to Larnach Castle, the only one in New Zealand.

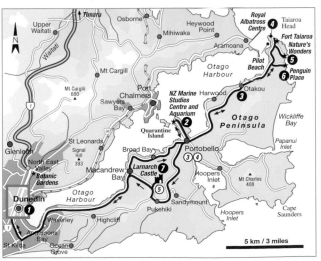

Birds of a feather
Albatross have nested at Taiaroa Head since 1914 and they share a unique bond with city's human inhabitants; every year when the albatrosses return after circumnavigating the southern oceans, church bells ring for one hour to let everyone know that the birds have made it safely home.

AKAROA

Spend a day discovering the Banks Peninsula and the attractive French-inspired settlement of Akaroa on this driving tour. Take a harbour cruise and enjoy a leisurely lunch overlooking the harbour before returning to Christchurch in the late afternoon.

DISTANCE 168km (104 miles) return
TIME A full day
START/END Christchurch
POINTS TO NOTE

You will need a car for this tour; for details of car-hire firms, *see p.111.*
If you leave early, there will be time to return to Christchurch via Summit Road, Diamond Harbour and Lyttelton, a scenic route that completes a loop around the Banks Peninsula.

Below: swing tyre at Lake Ellesmere.

Located around 80km (50 miles) from Christchurch, the little settlement of Akaroa began its European life in 1838, when a French whaler, Captain Jean-François Langlois, landed on its shores and bought – or so he thought – Banks Peninsula from the Maori. Sixty-three settlers set out from France on the *Comte de Paris* to create a South Seas outpost. But they arrived in 1840 to find the Union Jack flying. Pipped at the colonial post, the French settlers nevertheless stayed. They planted poplars from Normandy, named streets after places in their home country and grew grapes, but by 1843 they were outnumbered by the English.

The French dream lingers on, though, and has been brushed up for visitors. Little streets, with names such as Rue Lavaud and Rue Jolie, wind up the hill from the harbour front. A charming colonial style predominates, and has been protected by town-planning rules.

CHRISTCHURCH TO BARRY'S BAY

From Moorhouse Avenue in central **Christchurch ❶**, head west to where it connects with a corner of Hagley

Park. Follow the sign left into Lincoln Road (to **Lincoln** ❷), over the railway line and out on to what becomes SH75, travelling through the farmlands of Halswell, Taitapu and Motukarara.

Birdlings Flat

Here the road travels alongside Lake Ellesmere (Waihora), a wide, shallow coastal lagoon that attracts game birds and waterfowl, before taking a sharp turn left at the turn-off for **Birdlings Flat**. Take a short sidetrip here out to the beach, where the ocean transforms stones such as rose quartz into polished gems, and deposits them on the stony beach, ready to fossick. To see examples of the various precious gems that can be found on these shores, visit the local **Gemstone and Fossil Museum** (SH75; tel: 03 329 0812; www.bird lingsmuseum.741.com; Wed–Mon 9.30am–5pm; free).

Little River and Hilltop

Back on SH75 continue past picturesque Lake Forsyth to the small settlement of **Little River** ❸, once a notable stop on the old railway line through this part of the Banks Peninsula.

The road climbs steeply out of Cooptown up to **Hilltop** ❹ and the Hilltop Tavern, whose car park offers grand views over the Onawe Peninsula, which extends into the Akaroa Harbour. This was the site of a Maori *pa* (fortified village), built in 1831 by the Ngai Tahu people to stave off a northern tribe.

Barry's Bay

Descend into **Barry's Bay** ❺, where you can make a stop at Barry's Bay Cheese (Main Road, Barry's Bay; tel: 03 304 5809; www.barrysbaycheese. co.nz; daily 9am–5pm; free) to sample their traditionally hand-crafted products and watch the cheese-making process through glass windows, before travelling on through Duvauchelle and Takamatua to **Akaroa** ❻.

AKAROA

Park as soon as you enter the town – there's plenty of free parking available – and walk along Rue Lavaud.

Akaroa Museum

Make your first stop the **Akaroa Museum** (tel: 03 304 7614; daily 10.30am–4.30pm; charge), situated at the corner of Rue Lavaud and Rue Balguerie. Here, highlights include Maori *taonga* (treasures), as well as

Above from far left: the Akaroa Peninsula; French cuisine in Akaroa.

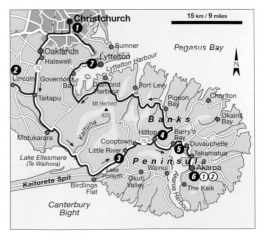

Above from left:
historic time-keeping;
sheep farmer and his
flock near Akaroa;
expect to see French
and English signs in
multilingual Akaroa.

relics from Akaroa's whaling past. A
20-minute audiovisual relates the
complete history of the town.

Langlois–Eteveneaux Cottage

The museum also incorporates several
of the town's important historical buildings, including the Customs House at
Daly's Wharf and the **Langlois-Eteveneaux Cottage** (corner of Rue Lavaud
and Rue Balguerie). The cottage, which
was prefabricated in France, is one of
the oldest in Canterbury.

Other Sights

After visiting the museum, take a walk
along Rue Balguerie to **St Patrick's**

Church, built in 1863, then continue
on up Rue Balgueri to Settlers Hill,
where a track will lead you to L'Aube
Hill Reserve and the **Old French
Cemetery**, the first consecrated burial
ground in Canterbury.

Next, return to Rue Lavaud and enjoy
a stroll through its gardens, past the cen-
trepiece **War Memorial** to the sweeping
beachside promenade. On a sunny day
it's lovely to walk around the bay to the
English part of town, taking in the views
across the inlet.

Alternatively, you can drive the same
route and park near the **Akaroa wharf**,
a popular place for fishing. For refreshments, try **L'Escargot Rouge**, see ⑪①.

Right: Akaroa
lighthouse.

Akaroa Harbour

It is now time to head for **Akaroa Harbour**. Sign up at the wharf for a harbour cruise aboard **Black Cat Cruises** (tel: 03 304 7641; www. blackcat.co.nz; daily Nov–Apr 11am and 1.30pm, May–Oct 1.30pm; charge), which explores Akaroa's deep, sea-filled crater.

On the two-hour trip to the headlands you will visit a salmon farm and spot dolphins, fur seals and a variety of sea birds, such as the little blue penguin. The company also provides the only opportunity in New Zealand to swim with the Hector's (or NZ) dolphin (Nov–Apr 6am, 8.30am, 11.30am, 1.30pm, 3.30pm, May–Oct 11.30am). This is one of the world's smallest and rarest dolphin species, with a total population of around 6,000–7,000 animals.

After the cruise, if the timing's right, take time out to sample the fresh catch of the day and the excellent local wines at cafés, including **Truby's Bar & Café**, see ⑪②, by the waterfront.

BACK TO CHRISTCHURCH

To return to Christchurch, there are two options: either retrace your route through Little River, Motukarara, Taitapu and Halswell or, for a two-hour scenic drive of Banks Peninsula, go back to Christchurch via the port township of **Lyttelton ❼**.

For the route through Lyttelton, take the signposted Summit Road, which offers gorgeous scenic views, but travels along an unsealed road with some sheer drop-offs. This route is not recommended for the vertiginous; nevertheless, those who do take it will be well rewarded visually. Depart with a near-full tank of petrol and follow the signs through the peaceful seaside settlements of Pigeon Bay, Diamond Harbour and Governor's Bay, and on through the Lyttelton tunnel back to Christchurch city centre.

Food and Drink

① L'ESCARGOT ROUGE
67 Beach Road, Akaroa; tel: 03 304 8774; $
Otherwise known as Akaroa's famous Deli to Go, L'Escargot Rouge dishes up delicious deli fare with a French twist – naturally. You will need to be there early, as its apricot custard Danish and pain au chocolat sell out fast.

② TRUBY'S BAR & CAFÉ
83 Rue Jolie, Akaroa; tel: 03 304 7707; $
There's no better place to eat Southern blue cod and chips than seated alfresco at Truby's on Akaroa's main beach.

Cheese Production

Cheese-making has a long history on Banks Peninsula. The earliest documented instances date from around 1844, when settlers used 'chessets' and presses on their farms in its production. The first shipment of cheese to leave the region was lost en route to Wellington, but, by the 1850s, Akaroa's Port Cooper cheese was a hit in Melbourne and sold for 2/6d a pound. It was a thriving industry, as New Zealand's burgeoning gold fields created a strong demand for locally made cheese, and by 1893, cheese factories were dotted all over the peninsula, from Little River to Okains Bay. Today, however, Barry's Bay Cheese is the only factory still operating on the peninsula; cheese-tastings are on offer here.

HANMER SPRINGS

This tour heads north of Christchurch through the farmland of the Canterbury Plains to the hot-springs resort of Hanmer. Visit Thrillseekers' Canyon, climb Conical Hill, walk the forests and enjoy a soak in the thermal pools.

DISTANCE 266km (165 miles)
TIME A full day
START Christchurch
END Hanmer Springs
POINTS TO NOTE

This trip can be done as a day tour from Christchurch or linked with the West Coast route on p.86.

Hanmer Hikes

There are lots of good short hiking trails around Hanmer, ranging from 20 minutes to two hours. The more energetic will enjoy the Mount Isobel Track, a six-hour return hike through larches and subalpine scrub to the summit of the mountain. The five-and-a-half-hour journey to Dog Stream Waterfall is also popular. Both hikes offer alternative routes on the return.

The alpine resort township of Hanmer Springs is located in the foothills of the Southern Alps, 135km (84 miles) north of Christchurch. Surrounded by vast tracts of indigenous forests in a landscape cut by sometimes meandering, sometimes roaring rivers, the road to Hanmer is a scenic one.

Driving nonstop to Hanmer Springs will take about two hours, but it's worth taking time en route to enjoy the Waipara Valley vineyards; here, pinot noir, riesling, chardonnay and sauvignon blanc grapes thrive in a warm microclimate, out of reach of the brisk easterly winds that swirl through the foothills.

TOWARDS WAIPARA

From central **Christchurch ❶**, travel north up Colombo Street to the intersection at Bealey Avenue. Turn right onto Bealey Avenue, then turn left on to

Bealey Avenue, then turn left on to Sherborne Street (SH74); follow it to Belfast, where it continues as SH1. Soon after you will cross the wide shingle river bed of the Waimakariri River, followed by the Ashley and Kowai rivers.

Cafés and Wineries

Approximately 6km (4 miles) beyond **Amberley** – home to the **Nor'Wester Café**, see ⑪①, if you need a pit stop – look out for the regimented rows of grapevines that mark the beginning of the Waipara Valley wine region, around **Waipara ❷**. There are several options if you want to break your journey at this point: try **The Mudhouse Winery**, see ⑪②, 8km (5 miles) north of Amberley, or the **Waipara Springs Winery**, see ⑪③, 4km (2½ miles) north of the Waipara Bridge. Both vineyards are easy to spot on the main drag.

For a more personal experience, follow the signposts to the highly acclaimed boutique winery of **Pegasus Bay**, see ⑪④, where you have a good chance of being introduced to its wines by the passionate wine makers themselves.

WAIKARI

To continue on your way, return to Waipara Junction just beyond the Waipara Bridge and turn off on to

SH7 (signposted to Lewis Pass). Drive through the birch-lined **Weka Pass** (named after an inquisitive native New Zealand bird) to **Waikari ❸**, the boarding point for the historic Weka Pass Railway, and nearby Maori Cave Art. Also of interest midway between Waikari and the township of Cul-

verden is the historic Hurunui Hotel, see ⑪⑤, built of limestone in 1868 to accommodate weary drovers. It has a peaceful garden bar and traditional pub atmosphere.

Look out for St Andrew's Church as you drive (still on SH7) through **Culverden ❹**, once a main rail terminus

Above from far left: cute kiwi; relaxing at Hanmer Springs; winemaking is big business in this part of the country.

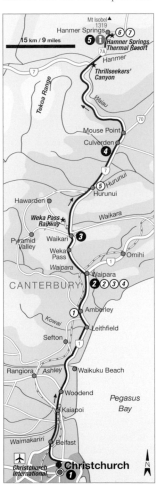

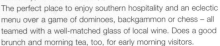

Food and Drink

① NOR'WESTER CAFÉ
Amberley; tel: 03 314 9411; $
The perfect place to enjoy southern hospitality and an eclectic menu over a game of dominoes, backgammon or chess – all teamed with a well-matched glass of local wine. Does a good brunch and morning tea, too, for early morning visitors.

② THE MUDHOUSE WINERY
780 Glasnevin Road (SH1), Waipara; tel: 03 314 6900; www.mudhouse.co.nz; $–$$
'Wild' pies are a speciality at Mudhouse; try 'Pigs in Mud' (wild boar), 'Billy the Kid' (wild but mild goat curry) and 'The Stag' (wild venison) – all of which team well with its own wines. For something a little tamer, the ploughman's is a good option.

③ WAIPARA SPRINGS WINERY
409 Omihi Road/SH1, Waipara; tel: 03 314 6777; www.waiparasprings.co.nz; $$
Located 4km (2½ miles) north of the Waipara Bridge, this winery offers a range of platters, plus an à la carte menu.

④ PEGASUS BAY WINERY
Stockgrove Road, Waipara; tel: 03 314 6869; www.pegasus bay.com; $$$
This family-owned operation is one of New Zealand's finest boutique wineries. Its sauvignon semillon, riesling, chardonnay, pinot noir and cabernet/merlot can be sampled at the tasting bar or matched to the menu, which uses local ingredients. Char-grilled Angus/Hereford beef fillet is offered with the vineyard's premium pinot noir. Recommended.

⑤ HURUNUI HOTEL
1224 Karaka Road (SH7), Culverden; tel: 03 314 4207; www.hurunuihotel.co.nz; $
A cosy and friendly family-run pub with an all-day bar menu. Game pies are a speciality and home-style meals available Thursday to Sunday with pizza on Wednesday only.

Above from left:
Waiau River; the
lakeside Church of
the Good Shepherd.

Below: hands-on
experience of Maori
crafts, using the
harakeke (flax) plant.

Historic Springs
The Maori knew of
Hanmer Springs long
before Europeans
came on the scene.
Their legends speak
of Tamatea, whose
canoe was wrecked
off the Otago coast.
To save his party from
freezing he called
upon the mountains
of Tongariro and
Ngauruhoe in the
north for help. They
sent flames down
the Whanganui River
and over to Nelson,
where they rose in
the air and landed
in Hanmer Springs.

but now a small town of fewer than 500
people, and, at the Waiau River, anglers
fishing for salmon and trout.

HANMER SPRINGS

About 126km (78 miles) from Christchurch is the SH7A turn off to **Hanmer
Springs** ❺. Make the turn, then look
for the car park 200m/yds ahead on your
right. Park here and go for a walk to see
dramatic views of Waiau River plunging
through Thrillseekers' Canyon.

A stroll leads to the 140-year-old
single-lane **Waiau Ferry Bridge,** which
still has its original steelwork intact; it
quickly becomes clear how this gorge
got its name. Bungy-jumpers leap from
here into the fast-flowing Waiau River;
jet-boat rides and whitewater rafting
trips are on offer too through **Thrillseekers** (Ferry Bridge; tel: 03 315 7046;
www.thrillseekerscanyon.co.nz; charge).
Continue to Hanmer, about 8km (5
miles) up the road.

As you enter town, make a stop at
the **Hurunui i-SITE Visitor Centre**
(42 Amuri Avenue West; tel: 0800 442
663; www.visithurunui.com; daily
9.30am–5pm), adjacent to the Hanmer
Springs Thermal Resort's hot pools.

Hikers should walk the half-hour
Zig-Zag Track up Conical Hill, just
behind the township, for fine views over
the Hanmer Basin. Walk up Conical
Hill Road to reach the start of the track,
calling in at **Mumbles**, see ⑪⑥, if you
need refreshment.

Hot Springs

As a relaxing alternative, or as a wind-
down after some of the more energetic
local activities, soak in the hot pools
at **Hanmer Springs Thermal Resort
& Spa** (Amuri Avenue; tel: 03 315
0000; www.hanmersprings.co.nz; daily
10am–9pm; charge), just east of the visitor information centre.

The springs were first used by ancient
Maori, stopping en route to the West
Coast to collect *pounamu* (jade).
Although they feature in ancient Maori
legends, the pools were only 'discovered'
by Europeans in 1859, and further
development was hindered by the inac-
cessibility of the region. The first iron
bathing shed was erected in 1879, and
in post-war years the recuperative
powers of the springs were used by the
nearby Queen Mary Hospital to assist
in the recovery of soldiers returning
from the war. There are now seven
open-air thermal pools, three sulphur
pools and four private pools, plus therapeutic massage or beauty treatments.

When you are feeling refreshed, pick
up a bite to eat at the **Hanmer Springs
Bakery**, see ⑪⑦, then either retrace
your way to Christchurch, or continue
through the beech-covered slopes of
the Lewis Pass to link up with the West
Coast tour *(see p.86).*

Food and Drink 🍴

⑥ MUMBLES CAFÉ
6 Conical Hill Road, Hanmer Springs; tel: 03 315 7124; $
Unpretentious home-cooked food served by friendly locals.

⑦ HANMER SPRINGS BAKERY
16 Conical Hill Road, Hanmer Springs; tel: 03 315 7714; $
Freshly made sandwiches, rolls and pies, plus great home-baking
such as Eccles cakes and enormous chocolate chip cookies.

CHRISTCHURCH TO QUEENSTOWN

A multi-day trip from Christchurch to Queenstown via Aoraki Mount Cook, New Zealand's highest mountain. Overnight at Aoraki Mount Cook Village, enjoy a flight above the Tasman Glacier and Southern Alps, then continue through the Mackenzie Country hinterland to Queenstown.

From **Christchurch ❶**, head south on SH1, travelling on the long straights of the plains of South Canterbury, a colourful patchwork of fields flanked by the dramatic peaks of the Southern Alps, crossing New Zealand's longest bridge over the Rakaia River.

Drive through **Ashburton**, then take the turn-off on to SH79 shortly after crossing the Rangitata River, where kayaks and whitewater rafts negotiate the wilder stretches of water.

GERALDINE

Geraldine ❷, on the banks of the Waihi River, is a good place to stop and stretch your legs. Popular with artisans, it's a hive of creativity. You can tempt your taste buds on Talbot Street, too, either at Talbot Forest Cheese (Four Peaks Plaza; tel: 03 693 1111), Barker Fruit Processors (Four Peaks Plaza; tel: 03 693 9727), Coco (10 Talbot Street; tel: 03 693 9982) or the **Verde Café**, see ⑪①. At the Giant Jersey (10 Wilson Street; tel: 03 693 9820; www.giantjersey.co.nz), gorgeously soft perendale, mohair and merino wools are crafted into stylish made-to-measure garments.

DISTANCE	491km (305 miles)
TIME	Two to three days
START	Christchurch
END	Queenstown

POINTS TO NOTE

You will need a car for this tour; for details of car-hire firms, *see p.111*. The drive from Christchurch to Aoraki Mount Cook covers 331km (206 miles) and will take about five to six hours with stops included. From Aoraki Mount Cook it is 262km (163 miles) to Queenstown; about another three to four hours on the road. The scenery, however, more than compensates.

FAIRLIE

Return to your vehicle and continue on SH79 to **Fairlie ❸**, the gateway to the Mackenzie Country, where huge oak trees provide shady relief

Flying Alternative

If you don't have time to drive but would still like to see the glaciers and peaks of the Southern Alps and Aoraki Mount Cook, the direct Air New Zealand flight from Christchurch to Queenstown offers spectacular views, weather permitting. Also note that depending on what time you plan to arrive, it's best to book ahead for a ski-plane flight to the glaciers and Aoraki Mount Cook with Mount Cook Ski Planes (*see p.85*).

Food and Drink

① VERDE CAFÉ

45 Talbot Street, Geraldine; tel: 03 693 9616; $
Set behind a white picket fence close to the river, this is a great coffee stop with sweet treats and an all-day brunch menu.

MAP ON P.84 •

Above from left:
view of Aoraki Mount
Cook from Lake
Pukaki; Church of
the Good Shepherd,
Lake Tekapo; statue
of Sir Edmund Hillary;
the Tasman Glacier.

for picnickers on the main street.
A quick stroll round town takes in
highlights such as its tiny Heritage
Museum (charge).

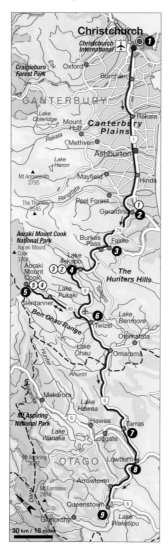

Country-style Cinema

Geraldine is not big
on nightlife but an
evening at its classic
country-style cinema
is unforgettable.
'Reverent Barry' (as
he's known around
town) greets every-
one at the door and
ushers you to your
seat – a cosy couch
downstairs, or a
regular seat up top.
Arthouse and
mainstream films are
screened on an old
Ermemanm Model II
projector, and an
interval is standard.

LAKE TEKAPO

You now begin the steep ascent past the
colonial homesteads of Burkes Pass,
and on through the Mackenzie
Country's striking vast plains to the
township of **Lake Tekapo ④**. The historic **Church of the Good Shepherd**,
built from locally gathered stones
as a memorial to the pioneers of
the Mackenzie Country, is a favourite
photo stop and offers grandstand views
of the lake, which is fed by glacier-melt
from the Alps. A solitary bronze
sheepdog stands guard nearby, in
honour of all high-country mustering
dogs. Try **Pepe's Pizza & Pasta** or
Kohan, see ⑪②–③, for a bite to eat.

Stop by the lake for a stretch and –
season permitting – consider spending
an hour skating or enjoying a spa at
Tekapo's lakeside **Alpine Springs Spa
& Winter Park** (6 Lakeside Drive; tel:
03 680 6550; www.winterpark.co.nz;
daily, spa 10am–9pm, winter park 10am
–9.30pm; charge), before continuing on
to **Lake Pukaki** to enjoy the dramatic
views of **Aoraki Mount Cook** across its
shimmering waters.

AORAKI MOUNT COOK VILLAGE

Further on, turn off onto SH80 for the
stunning 55km (34-mile) drive
beneath Ben Ohau's textured peaks to
Glentanner, where the lake meets glacial river rubble. From here a vast
valley of earthy tones and charcoal-
coloured scree slopes leads to **Aoraki
Mount Cook Village ⑤**. If you love

the great outdoors, there's lots to do here, and you may want to stay for several days *(see p.117)*. For dining options, see ⑪④–⑤.

Here, you are within the Aoraki Mount Cook National Park, and the local visitor centre has up-to-date information on the park's geology, climate, flora and fauna. There are lots of walks from the village, ranging from ten minutes to four hours in length. A must-do is the 30-minute hike to the Tasman Glacier viewpoint. Alternatively, join a Glacier Explorers boat adventure to see where the glacier yields its ice-melt to the glacier lake, before being washed away downstream.

Aoraki Mount Cook

The **Aoraki Mount Cook** is New Zealand's highest mountain, at 3,764m (12,348ft). From the small **airport** on SH80 you can fly with Mount Cook Ski Planes (tel: 03 435 1026; www.mt cookskiplanes.co.nz; daily, half-hourly departure; charge) to view some of the most awe-inspiring scenery in New Zealand. Land at the head of the Tasman Glacier – no ice axes or crampons required – or consider heli-skiing or Alpine Guides' 'Ski the Tasman' package (Sir Edmund Hillary Centre, Hermitage Hotel; tel: 03 435 1834; www.alpineguides.co.nz; daily) to get up close and personal with the gentle bowls, open snowfields, towering seracs and icefalls of the national park.

ON TO QUEENSTOWN

To reach Queenstown, go back to SH80 and drive south on SH8 past **Twizel** ❻ and **Tarras** ❼. After **Lowburn** ❽, take the turn-off right for SH6 and continue into **Queenstown** ❾.

Sir Edmund Hillary

Edmund Percival Hillary was born in Auckland in 1919. On 29 May 1953, he and Nepalese Sherpa mountaineer Tenzing Norgay became the first climbers known to have reached Mount Everest's summit, on a British expedition led by John Hunt. In his later years, Hillary devoted much of his time to humanitarian and conservation work and is respected as much in his native New Zealand for this as for his conquest of Everest. He died in Auckland in 2008. He graces the country's $5 bill.

Food and Drink

② PEPE'S PIZZA & PASTA
Main Street, Tekapo; tel: 03 680 6677; $$
In a niche of its own among the many fine-dining establishments along Tekapo's ridge, Pepe's offers great value for money, an ambient atmosphere with fireside dining and a cosy bar, and incredibly good pizza.

③ KOHAN JAPANESE RESTAURANT
SH8, Tekapo; tel: 03 680 688; $
The cooks at this popular Japanese restaurant know how to make good use of fresh locally farmed salmon. The best sashimi and sushi in the South Island is served here, along with teriyaki and tempura.

④ PANORAMA RESTAURANT
The Hermitage Hotel, Aoraki Mount Cook Village; tel: 03 435 1809; $$–$$$
Executive chef Franz Blum uses the freshest produce, sourced locally and from around New Zealand to prepare superb cuisine. Incredible views over the mountains. The hotel *(see p.117)* also houses the Snowline Bar.

⑤ CHAMOIS BAR
Aoraki Mount Cook Village; tel: 03 435 1809; $
This is the locals' favourite place to enjoy a hearty, home-style pub meal of mammoth proportions.

ARTHUR'S PASS AND THE WEST COAST

This three-day driving tour provides an alternative route from Christchurch to Queenstown, travelling from the Pacific Coast, through Arthur's Pass in the Southern Alps, to the Tasman Sea. The scenery is breathtaking all the way to Franz Josef and Fox glaciers, and beyond.

Jade Route

Maori first used Arthur's Pass on journeys to gather precious *pounamu* (jade) on the West Coast. Settlers later opened a road across the Canterbury Plains, up Porters Pass and into the Waimakariri Basin, which was used to carry dray-loads of wool to Christchurch from the inland sheep stations. When gold was discovered on the West Coast, the provincial government provided funds to extend the road through Arthur's Pass to the goldfields. One thousand men were employed, and the road was built in less than a year.

DISTANCE 754km (468 miles)

TIME Three days

START Christchurch

END Queenstown

POINTS TO NOTE

You will need a car for this tour; for details of car hire, see p.111. Bring warm clothes, sensible shoes and a torch for the cave visit detailed below.

The 260km (160-mile) route over the scenic Arthur's Pass to Hokitika on the West Coast provides one of the country's great geographical contrasts. This alpine highway climbs through a visual feast of mirrored lakes, caves and rock formations, ridges and valleys, wide shingle river beds and deep gorges.

CHRISTCHURCH TO LAKE LYNDON

From central **Christchurch ❶**, head south on Colombo Street; follow the road for three blocks and turn right on to Tuam Street. Continue to Christchurch Hospital and then drive into Hagley Park on Riccarton Avenue. Follow this all the way through the suburb of Riccarton, then veer right on to Yaldhurst Road, following the signposts for Arthur's Pass on to SH73.

This route takes you through the town of **Darfield ❷** , where **Terrace**, see ⑪①, is an option if you're hungry. From Darfield, continue on towards **Sheffield** and then **Springfield**, 70km (43½ miles) from Christchurch. SH73 climbs swiftly beyond Springfield into the foothills of the Southern Alps. At the same time, the scenery becomes increasingly dramatic.

Follow the road over **Porter's Pass** (923m/3028ft), which passes **Lake Lyndon** and the turn-off to Porter's Pass skifield, before you go past Kura Tawhiti (Castle Hill Reserve). **Cave Stream Scenic Reserve** is about 6km (4 miles) further on, and has a car park with good views of the basin area.

Cave Visit

Unless you suffer from claustrophobia, spend an hour exploring the 362m (1,188ft) limestone cave here, with its flowing stream and Maori cave art. You will need warm clothes, a torch with spare batteries, and a change of clothes for when you exit the cave.

ARTHUR'S PASS VILLAGE

SH73 passes **Lake Pearson** (pull into the rest area on the right for access to this lake), **Lake Grassmere** and **Lake Sarah**, before meeting up with the braided Waimakariri River. About 40km (25 miles) beyond Castle Hill is the **Bealey Hotel ❸**, see ⑪② and *p.117*, built when the road opened in 1866 to accommodate Cobb and Co. passengers on the three-day stage-coach journey to the West Coast. It is still an option if you want to stay overnight.

Another 10km (6 miles) and you will arrive in **Arthur's Pass Village ❹**, set in a bush-covered river valley among the mountains in the Arthur's Pass National Park. On the left heading into the village, there is a **visitor centre** (daily 8am–5pm; tel: 03 318 9211) with displays on local flora and fauna, and a video clip recalling the story of the first pass crossing. There is also information on a variety of walks in the area. Time permitting, you could hike the 2km (1¼-mile) track known as **Devil's Punch Bowl**, which leads to the base of a 131m (430ft) waterfall.

Above from far left: West Coast beach; helicopter flights over Aoraki Mount Cook offer spectacular views.

Below: views of Shantytown *(see p.88).*

Food and Drink ⑪

① TERRACE CAFÉ & BAR
20 Main South Terrace, Darfield; 03 318 7303; $-$$
Seasonal menu featuring locally reared meat (Canterbury lamb) and local salmon.

② BEALEY HOTEL
SH73, Arthur's Pass; tel: 03 318 9277; $
Hearty pub meals served in a magnificent mountain setting. See also p.117.

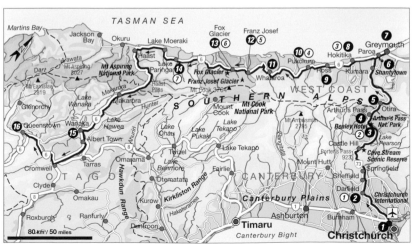

OTIRA

Leaving the village, the road climbs steeply for 4km (2½ miles) to the pass (912m/2,992ft), where you can pull into a signposted lookout on the right for glorious views and the company of a cheeky, green native kea (parrot).

From here the road descends steeply via the modern Otira Viaduct into the old railway township of **Otira ❺**. You are now on the West Coast – known in New Zealand as the Wild West Coast or sometimes the Wet Coast; the hardy locals are proud of the pristine condition of their precious rainforests, and the climate that keeps them that way.

Below: rugged West Coast beach.

SHANTYTOWN

While Maori journeyed to the West Coast for *pounamu* (jade), European settlers came for gold. A good way to experience those days of old is at **Shantytown ❻** (tel: 0800 742 689; www.shantytown.co.nz; daily 8.30am–5pm; charge). To get there, follow SH73 through the town of **Kumara** and then on to Kumara Junction. At the junction, head north on SH6, following the signs to Greymouth, turning off at **Paroa**, and follow the signs to Shantytown.

Highlights

This replica West Coast settlement has more than 30 historic buildings to see, including a sawmill, stables, bank, hotel, barber's shop, miners' hall, printing works and blacksmith. You can take a ride on a steam train (departs hourly throughout the day), including the 25-tonne *Kaitangata* built in 1897, on tracks that follow the route of an old sawmill tramline. Like many of the first bush tramways in New Zealand, this historic route was originally wooden-railed and worked by horses. You can also try your hand at panning for alluvial gold here.

Food and Drink 🍴

③ CAFÉ DE PARIS
19–21 Tancred Street, Hokitika;
tel: 03 755 8933; $
A French-inspired café serving good coffee and mouth-watering cakes, and featuring a range of mains and desserts on its blackboard menu.

GREYMOUTH

It's another 10km (6 miles) north into **Greymouth** ❼, where highlights include the **Jade Boulder Gallery** (1 Guinness Street; tel: 03 768 0700; daily 9am–5.30pm; free), a museum that tells the story of this semiprecious stone, and **Monteith's Brewery** (60 Herbert Street; tel: 03 768 4149; www. monteiths.co.nz; charge), a classic West Coast icon, offering tours of the plant followed by a tasting.

HOKITIKA

If you're planning to stay overnight on this part of the coast, it's worth backtracking on SH6 and continuing 40km (25 miles) south to **Hokitika** ❽, as the distances to other attractions further south make this the perfect night stop. For details of hotels, *see p.118*. There isn't much to do in this town in the evenings, except catch a movie at the Regent cinema (23 Weld Street; tel: 03 755 8101; www.hokitikaregent.com) or admire glow-worms in the signposted dell 1km (²/₃ mile) north on SH6. Alternatively, dine at **Café de Paris**, see ⑪③.

West Coast Historical Museum

In the morning visit the **West Coast Historical Museum** (tel: 03 755 6898; summer daily 9.30am–5pm, winter Mon–Fri 9.30am–5pm, Sat–Sun 10am–2pm; charge), accessed via the Hokitika Visitor Centre (Carnegie Building, corner of Tancred and Hamilton streets; tel: 03 755 6166).

The museum mounts an audiovisual show telling the story of the West Coast gold rushes. In 1864, Hokitika grew almost overnight into a major commercial area and one of New Zealand's busiest ports, despite the treacherous sandbar that claimed 32 ships between 1865 and 1867. The kumara rush marked the end of a golden age, and most fortune-seekers drifted off to try their luck elsewhere.

Pick up local maps at the museum and take a walk around town, combining your tour with an exploration of the jade galleries and studios of Hokitika's many artisans, who include glassblowers, jewellers, woodturners and potters.

JOURNEY TO THE GLACIERS

There is a lot of driving to do today, so don't linger for too long in Hokitika. Fill up with petrol (gas), make sure you've got some cash or a credit card to hand because there are no banks until you get to Wanaka or Queenstown, and head south on SH6 to the glaciers 148km (92 miles) further down the coast.

Ross

On the way you will pass through the town of **Ross** ❾, where the largest gold nugget in New Zealand was unearthed in 1909. It weighed 3.6kg (7.9lb) and was presented to King George V as a coronation present. The **Ross Goldfields Information and Heritage Centre** (4 Aylmer Street; tel: 03 755 4077; www.ross.org.nz; daily 9am–4pm; charge) gives details on the area's history.

Above from far left: the TranzAlpine Express Train en route to Greymouth; West Coast forest; the coast in this area is famous for its whitebait (the season runs Sept–Nov).

West Coast Rocks Punakaiki has 'pancake rocks' (limestone formations that look like towers of giant flapjacks) and surf blowholes.

Hiking the Glacier

Franz Josef Glacier Guides (SH6, Franz Josef; tel: 03 752 0763; www.franzjosefglacier.com) provide access to a unique hiking experience: tramping on Franz Josef, the world's steepest and fastest-flowing commercially guided glacier. Specially designed ice shoes are strapped on over your boots. At first the ice shoes feel ungainly, but, before long, your speed picks up, and you should be walking on the glacier like a pro.

Pukekura

Drive another 25km (15½ miles) further south and watch out for the giant sandfly sculpture that marks the small settlement of **Pukekura** ⑩. Stop off at the **Bushman's Museum and Bushman's Centre** (tel: 03 755 4144; www.pukekura.co.nz; daily 9am–5pm; charge) for an entertaining insight into West Coast life. Refreshments can be enjoyed at the **Bushman's Centre Café**, see ⑪④.

Towards Whataroa

Continue another 4km (2½ miles) past the serene shores of trout-filled **Lake Ianthe**, and on through **Harihari** to **Whataroa** ⑪, the renowned breeding grounds of the graceful and rare *kotuku*, or white heron. Access to its breeding grounds is restricted to group trips run by White Heron Sanctuary

Tours (tel: 03 753 4120; www.whiteherontours.co.nz; charge). *See also margin opposite.*

FRANZ JOSEF VILLAGE AND GLACIER

Shortly after driving past **Lake Mapourika** (famous for its trout and salmon), you will arrive at the village of **Franz Josef** ⑫, home of the magnificent **Franz Josef Glacier**. Your first stop should be the **visitor centre** (SH6; tel: 03 752 0796; daily 8.30am–5pm), for maps and to view its extremely informative display on the history, geology and ecology of the glacier region. For half- and full-day guided tours walking on the ice of Franz Josef Glacier, contact Franz Josef Glacier Guides (tel: 03 752 0763; www.franzjosefglacier.com; daily

---

Food and Drink 🍴

④ BUSHMAN'S CENTRE CAFÉ
SH6, Pukekura; tel: 03 755 4144; $
This wild West Coast café presents an amusing menu of local fare, from tasty 'Roadkill Pies', featuring possum, venison, goat and rabbit meat, to vegetarian 'Grasseater' sandwiches.

⑤ CHEEKY KEA
Main Road, Franz Josef Village; tel: 03 752 0139; $
Affordable casual dining, with burgers, toasties, nachos, salads, curries and a range of pre-prepared cabinet food.

⑥ CAFÉ NEVE
Main Road, Fox Glacier; tel: 03 751 0110; $$
A friendly café/restaurant serving a variety of cuisine, including award-winning beef and lamb, seafood, venison and gourmet pizza.

⑦ SALMON FARM CAFÉ
SH6, Paringa; tel: 03 751 0837; $–$$
Sample freshly hooked farmed salmon (catch your own if you wish!) and hot smoked salmon at this farm café.

7.30am–8pm; charge). There are also scenic plane rides and helicopter flights to Franz Josef and/or Fox glaciers, as well as scenic flights to Aoraki Mount Cook.

If you prefer to take a look at the glacier on your own, drive over the **Waiho River** and turn left, driving a further 5km (3 miles) into the car park. From here a 90-minute walk along a 4km (2½-mile) trail from the car park will bring you face to face with this giant river of ice. However, without crampons or strap-on ice shoes (provided on the tour), the glacier itself is too slippery and dangerous to explore on foot.

There's a range of accommodation available in Franz Josef; for details, *see p.119.* Most of the modern places to stay are located on Cron Street, opposite the new **Glacier Hot Pools** (tel: 0800 044 044; www.glacierhotpools. co.nz; daily noon–10pm; charge), where a series of private and public pools is set amid the rainforest. A good place to eat in the village is the **Cheeky Kea**, see ⑪⑤.

FOX GLACIER VILLAGE AND GLACIER

The village of **Fox Glacier** ⑬, 25km (15½ miles) to the south, is smaller than Franz Josef. **Café Neve**, see ⑪⑥, is a good option for a bite to eat.

To get to the glacier itself, drive through the town and turn left on to Glacier Road. You'll reach a car park after 6km (4 miles), and from there it is a 30-minute walk to the face of

the glacier. If you prefer a guided tour, book direct with Fox Glacier Guiding (tel: 03 751 0825; www.foxguides. co.nz). Time and weather permitting, take a short detour to Lake Matheson from town, following the signs off SH6 to see views of the summit of Aoraki Mount Cook and Fox Glacier mirrored in the still waters of the lake. Weather-wise, the early morning is the best time to visit.

If you choose to stay overnight in Fox Glacier, *see p.119* for accommodation.

PARINGA

From Fox Glacier, continue south on SH6 through Kahikatea Forest past **Lake Paringa** ⑭ (look out for the excellent **Salmon Farm Café**, see ⑪⑦, if you want to stop on the way) and Lake Moeraki.

ON TO QUEENSTOWN

To reach Queenstown there is a lot of distance to cover (267km/166 miles to Wanaka and 338km/210 miles to Queenstown), driving through the magnificent Haast Pass in the **Mount Aspiring National Park**. Keep on SH6 all the way. Here towering peaks surround vast open valleys and lofty waterfalls plunge from steep green cliffs. Make a stop at the spectacular 'Gates of Haast' bridge before continuing on to **Wanaka** ⑮, a pleasant town with an attractive lake and good watersports facilities. From here continue on SH6 to **Queenstown** ⑯.

Above from far left: view into an ice cave on the Franz Josef Glacier; the top of the Franz Josef Glacier; alpine sign.

Heron Colony
White Heron Sanctuary Tours provide access to New Zealand's only nesting colony of the white heron via jet-boat, which travels down the Waitangitaona and Waitangiroto rivers, through towering kahikatea forest to a small jetty. From there, boardwalks lead past a series of predator traps and through native kotukutuku, makomako and miro trees to a screened viewing platform. The first herons arrive at these breeding grounds in early September, and, after courtship, nest high above the water. From the viewing platform you can spy on their nests and watch them feed their chicks with food from the nearby Okarito Lagoon (SH6, Whataroa; tel: 0800 523 456; www.white herontours.co.nz).

QUEENSTOWN

It's easy to see why Queenstown is unashamedly a tourist town, given its location in an area of spectacular natural beauty. There is a huge range of leisure activities on offer and great shopping. This tour, encompassing gondola rides, bungy-jumping and jet-boat rides, covers its highlights.

Maori History

In the early days Central Otago was the great divide that the Maori had to cross in order to access the greenstone, or *pounamu*, from the mountains of the West Coast. The stone was often used to make *tiki*, Polynesian amulets in the shape of a human figure, believed to be endowed with *mana* or power.

DISTANCE 14km (8 miles)
TIME A full day
START Queenstown i-SITE Visitor Centre
END Queenstown Gardens
POINTS TO NOTE

A number of activities are recommended as part of this tour. During the summer it's best to book these in advance to avoid disappointment.

Resting on the shore of Lake Wakatipu, with mountains looming all around and valleys cut deep by swift-flowing rivers, Queenstown in Central Otago is the quintessential year-round holiday resort. It has grown from a sleepy lakeside town into a sophisticated all-year tourist attraction. Within a radius of only a few kilometres, the ingenuity and mechanical wizardry of New Zealanders have combined with the stunning landscape to provide an unrivalled range of adventure activities. Little wonder, then, that the city is often dubbed the 'Adventure Capital of the World'.

SKYLINE GONDOLA

Begin your day at the **Queenstown i-SITE Visitor Centre ❶** (Clocktower Building, corner Shotover and Camp streets; tel: 03 442 4100; www.queenstown-vacation.com; daily, summer 7.30am–6.30pm, winter 7.30am–6pm; free). Here you can pick up maps and brochures outlining the vast range of outdoor pursuits available in Queenstown. For a great breakfast nearby, head to **Joe's Garage**, see ⑪①.

Walk northwest up Camp Street, make a left into Isle Street, then the first right into Brecon Street, home to the **Skyline Gondola ❷** (tel: 03 441 0101; www.skyline.co.nz; daily 9am–late; charge). The gondola rises some 450m (1,476ft) up Bob's Peak to a magnificent view of Queenstown, Lake Wakatipu and The Remarkables mountain range.

At the top, a walking track leads to the base for an activity that has become a New Zealand icon – bungy-jumping. This particular operation is called The

---

Food and Drink 🍴

① JOE'S GARAGE
Searle Lane; tel: 03 442 5282; daily 7am–3pm; $
With its strong coffee focus, Joe's Garage has built up street cred with its breakfast/brunch menu.

② PIER 19
Steamer Wharf; tel: 03 442 4006; $–$$
This swish café/bar is right on the lake – any further and you'd get wet – and the perfect place to relax on a hot day. Crayfish, whitebait and oysters are often on the menu.

Ledge and is run by bungy pioneer A.J. Hackett (tel: 03 441 8926; www.bungy. co.nz; daily, summer noon–7pm, winter 3–9pm). It offers spectacular views of Queenstown – if you manage to keep your eyes open – as you take the plunge.

Speed demons can ride the chairlifts to a higher elevation and take the **Luge** (daily from 10am until late, weather dependent; charge), a thrilling ride down the mountainside.

If you like the idea of flitting between trees, check in at the Ziptrek Ecotours (tel: 03 441 2102; www.zip trek.com; daily; charge) tree hut, near the gondola station, to ride a series of flying foxes which 'zip' between treetop platforms constructed high in the forest canopy.

CADDYSHACKS AND KIWIS

Returning on the gondola to Brecon Street, you have the opportunity to visit **Caddyshack City ❸** (tel: 03 442 6642; daily 10am–7pm; charge), an elaborate mini-golf centre, and the Kiwi Birdlife Park (Brecon Street; tel: 03 442 8059; www.kiwibird.co.nz; daily 9am–6pm; charge), an ideal place to spot kiwis of the feathered kind, if you haven't already. Time your visit to coincide with the 10am or 3pm conservation show, and kiwi feeding sessions held at 10am, noon, 1.30pm and 4.30pm.

STEAMER WHARF

Back on Brecon Street, walk downhill and turn right at Shotover Street and follow the road around to the **Steamer**

Wharf Village ❹, where there are shops and restaurants, including the lakefront **Pier 19**, see ⑪②.

The wharf is also home to a variety of vessels, but none so distinctive as the TSS *Earnslaw (see p.94)*, which was launched in 1912 and is affectionately known to locals as 'The Lady of the Lake'. The coal-fired boilers belch the *Earnslaw*'s trademark black smoke as she carries passengers on sightseeing tours. Book your cruise tickets with Real Journeys (Steamer Wharf; tel: 03 442 7500; www.realjourneys.co.nz; daily, departures every two hours 10am–8pm; charge) for the 2pm excursion to Walter Peak *(see p.94)*.

Above from far left: Lake Wakatipu; bungy-jumping at Bob's Peak; Kawarau Suspension Bridge; the Remarkables.

Lord of the Rings

The Queenstown region was used for numerous scenes in the *Lord of the Rings* movies. Many are, however, inaccessible without a helicopter ride. Taking one of several 'Rings' tours gets over this problem: see www.trilogy trail.com for details.

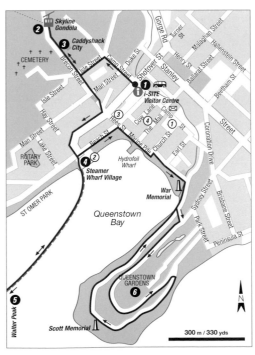

Above from left:
cruising on the
Earnslaw; jet-boat
on the Shotover River;
golden nuggets –
the reason for Arrow-
town's development
in the 19th century;
the Remarkables and
Lake Wakatipu.

Whitewater Rafting
The rugged beauty
and unspoilt grand-
eur of the upper
reaches of the
Shotover River also
provide the setting for
extreme whitewater-
rafting excitement;
the slightly tamer
Kawarau River pro-
vides an exhilarating
ride and a great
introduction to white-
water rafting for first-
time rafters. There
are four rapids to
negotiate, including
the final (unforgettable)
400m (1,312ft) Dog
Leg rapid. Kawarau
rafters will gain an
unusual perspective
of bungy-jumpers
plummeting from
the Kawarau
Suspension Bridge.

SHOTOVER JET-BOAT RIDE

Before then, though, there's an option to fit in some more action in the form of a jet-boat ride. Shotover Jets (Gorge Road, Arthur's Point; tel: 03 442 8570; www.shotoverjet.co.nz; daily, boats depart every 15 mins) operate on the Shotover River, 6km (4 miles) from town. A courtesy bus departs from Queenstown i-SITE Visitor Centre (corner Shotover and Camp streets), every 15 minutes. The jet-boat drivers are highly skilled, and their sense of humour can be gauged by the smiles on their faces as they spin you within centimetres of overhanging rocks. The boat ride only takes 30 minutes, but allow another hour for the ride to the river and back.

CAVELL MALL

On your return you may want to get your 'land legs' back by wandering around the waterfront and **Cavell Mall** area. Although much of Queenstown's architecture is contemporary, some of its attractive original buildings are still standing, including the former Eichardts' pub (1871) on Marine

Parade – now a lodge and stylish bar – and the courthouse and library buildings, built in 1876, at the corner of Ballarat and Stanley streets.

Habebe's and **Avanti**, see ⑪③–④, are good pit stops in this area.

EARNSLAW CRUISE

As 2pm draws near, make your way back to the wharf for your three-hour cruise on the TSS *Earnslaw* to **Walter Peak** ❺. On the western shore of the lake, Walter Peak is the original homestead of one of New Zealand's most famous sheep and cattle stations. The cruise across takes about 40 minutes, leaving you plenty of time to enjoy the gardens surrounding the homestead as well as watch a sheep-shearing demonstration and admire the herd of Scottish Highland cattle.

QUEENSTOWN GARDENS

Return to Queenstown and round the day off with a late-afternoon stroll around **Queenstown Gardens** ❻ (free) on the far side of Queenstown Bay. To get there, walk around past the jetty and along Marine Parade to the War Memorial, on a tree-lined promenade just behind the beachfront. Beyond it, a pathway leads into the gardens. Look out for the dramatic memorial to Antarctic explorer Robert Falcon Scott.

Circling back, you will gain views of Kelvin Heights, then of Walter Peak. This is a great place to watch the sunset, before returning along the beachfront and walking back into town.

Food and Drink

③ HABEBE'S
Wakatipu Arcade, Rees Street; tel: 03 442 9861; $
A favourite with Queenstowners for quick lunchtime wraps,
yummy vegetarian dishes and super fresh salads.

④ AVANTI
20 The Mall; tel: 03 442 8503; $
A great range of Italian dishes served inside or out.

ARROWTOWN

This tour is a drive over the Shotover Gorge, through Arthur's Point and up to Coronet Peak for a panoramic view of the Wakatipu Basin, before ascending to picturesque historic Arrowtown, a former gold-mining town.

A trip to Arrowtown, 21km (13 miles) from Queenstown, is a journey into the region's past. Situated in a quiet, leafy gully, the town played a prominent role in the gold-rush days of the 1860s, attracting fortune-seekers from around the world. As the gold diminished, so did Arrowtown's importance. It did not, however, go the way of desolation like so many other gold-mining settlements in the vicinity, slipping instead into a quieter way of life and revelling in its beautiful location.

QUEENSTOWN TO CORONET PEAK

In **Queenstown ❶**, turn left at the northern end of Shotover Street into Gorge Road. Continue for around 6km (4 miles), travelling past **Arthur's Point Tavern**. Some 500m/yds further on is the historic **Edith Cavell Bridge** *(see right)*, which spans the Shotover River. If you missed out on taking a jet-boat ride in Tour 16, take the first turn left into the car park at Shotover Jets (Gorge Road, Arthur's Point; tel: 03 442 8570; www.shotoverjet.co.nz; daily, boats depart every 15 minutes). Otherwise continue on the same route (it becomes Malaghans Road), passing Arthur's Point campsite on your right and the Moonlight Country stables

| DISTANCE 83km (51 miles) |
| TIME A half-day |
| START/END Queenstown |
| POINTS TO NOTE |
| You will need a car for this tour; for details of car hire, *see p.111.* This trip includes a stop at a vineyard; note the local rules on drink/driving *(see p.65).* |

(Domain Road; tel: 03 442 1240; www.moonlightcountry.co.nz; charge) on your left, where 90-minute horse rides are available for beginners through to advanced riders.

Slow down as you pass the luxury lodge **Distinction Nugget Point** (146 Arthur's Point Road; tel: 03 441 0288; www.distinctionqueenstown.co.nz), because just beyond on the left is the turn-off to **Coronet Peak** and **Skippers Canyon**. The latter is off limits to most rental cars owing to its treacherous nature. Should you wish to explore, Nomad Safaris (tel: 03 442 6699; www.nomadsafaris.co.nz; daily 8.30am, 1.30pm; charge) offer guided tours.

However, Coronet Peak, a top-class ski-field in the winter, is easily accessible with a fully sealed mountain road of around 20km (12¹⁄₂ miles); allow 40 minutes for the return trip. Here, every year in early July, Coronet Peak

Edith Cavell

Born in 1865 to a clergyman and his wife in Norfolk, England, Cavell is known for her extraordinary achievements as a nurse and humanitarian. A nurse during World War I, she helped hundreds of Allied soldiers to escape from occupied Belgium to the neutral Netherlands. She was arrested in 1915 and executed on 12 October. The Edith Cavell Bridge over the Shotover River is one of many memorials named in her honour.

Prime Skiing

In the winter, the Southern Lakes region of the South Island is transformed into a magical wonderland, with perfect powder snow covering the slopes of the surrounding mountain ranges. There are four ski-fields within easy access of Queenstown and Wanaka: Coronet Peak, Cardrona, Treble Cone and the Remarkables.

Dorothy Browns
Arrowtown is home to one of New Zealand's quirkiest movie houses, Dorothy Browns Cinema, Bar and Bookshop (tel: 03 442 1968; www. dorothybrowns.com) on Buckingham Street. This charming boutique cinema shows arthouse films (check online for the schedule) and has unusually large, comfortable seating, an open fire and a bar. It is apparently named after a turn-of-the-century photographer, who lived with one of the Chinese workers from the local gold-mining community.

comes alive during the **Queenstown Winter Festival** (tel: 0800 3378 4825; www.winterfestival.co.nz; charge). Celebrity skiers, sheepdog trials, night skiing and all-night partying signal the start of the ski season in the region. But no matter the season, it is a superb place to enjoy wide-ranging views of the Wakatipu Basin. From here you can see the rugged **Remarkables**, a jagged mountain range that drops dramatically down to Lake Wakatipu.

ARROWTOWN

Back at the bottom of the mountain, turn left on to Malaghans Road and resume your journey to **Arrowtown ②**, watching out for **Millbrook Resort** (Malaghans Road, Arrowtown; tel: 03 441 7000; www.millbrook.co.nz; *see*

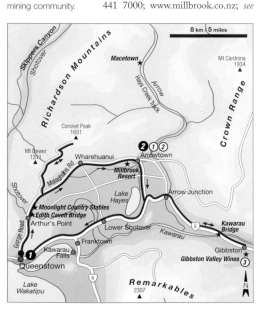

p.118), a stylish hotel complex with an 18-hole golf course designed by one of New Zealand's top golfers, left-hander Bob Charles. It's also your cue to take the next left on to Berkshire Street, which leads into Arrowtown.

Buckingham Street

Leave the car for a while and take a stroll down Buckingham Street, which has the look and feel of a Hollywood movie set and is especially beautiful in autumn. Here you will find artisan stores and souvenir shops, as well as a number of historic landmarks recalling this small town's rich history, among them a monument to the Chinese gold-miners who played an important role in the development of the region.

Those seeking souvenirs of the golden kind should call into **The Gold Shop** (29 Buckingham Street; tel: 03 442 1319; www.thegoldshop.co.nz; daily), which sells jewellery and nuggets. Just beyond The Gold Shop is a map and information board about Arrowtown, with a potted history of the region.

For a more 'hands-on' historical experience, head to the **Lakes District Museum** (49 Buckingham Street; tel: 03 442 1824; www.museumqueens town.com; daily 8.30am–5pm; charge). When your history lesson concludes, cross the street to **The Red Tractor**, see ⑪①, or head to the **Arrowtown Bakery & Café**, see ⑪②.

Further along, located on what is known as the 'Avenue of Trees' (the willow- and sycamore-lined end of Buckingham Street), is a row of old miners' cottages, Arrowtown's library

and beyond that the old schist-built Masonic Lodge and original jail.

Panning for Gold

If you are feeling lucky, a great way to spend half an hour or so is to hire a gold-pan (available from the information centre at the Lakes District Museum; 49 Buckingham Street; daily 8.30am–5pm) and try your hand at gold-panning. Just below the village, beyond a long line of car parks, is the Arrow River, where with a bit of time and effort you have a decent chance of garnering a few gold flakes.

Arrowtown Chinese Camp

Another way to gain insight into the hardships of mining a century ago is to walk to the **Arrowtown Chinese Camp** (daily; free), located on the high river bank, near where you entered town. Plum and berry trees surround these hillside huts. Check out Ah-Lums Store at the beginning of the walkway and the humorous Historic Places classification given to an old toilet.

BACK TO QUEENSTOWN

There are several routes out of Arrow-town, but we suggest driving back along Berkshire Street and, instead of turning into Malaghans Road, continue straight on into Arrowtown/Lake Hayes Road for a scenic drive past Lake Hayes. At the junction with SH6, turn left and travel for 10km (6 miles), until you reach the Kawarau Bridge, the site of A.J. Hackett's first commercial bungy-jump operation (SH6, Queenstown; tel: 03 442 5356; www.bungy.co.nz; daily

summer 9am–5.30pm, winter 9.30am–5pm; charge), an option for thrill-seeking visitors.

Gibbston Valley Wines

For a relaxing end to the day head to **Gibbston Valley Wines** (SH6, Queenstown; tel: 03 442 6910; www.gvwines.co.nz), see 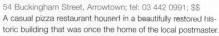, a further 5km (3 miles) along SH6. Tours (charge) are held on the hour through the vineyard and winery, and finish with a wine tasting.

Although the vineyard's focus is on its internationally recognised pinot noir, other attractions, such as Gibbston Valley Cheesery, where small batches are made with flavours changing subtly with the seasons, are popular. You can sample cheese, then purchase a platter to complement a wine-tasting tray and enjoy it alfresco on tables overlooking the valley, or inside beside a roaring fire.

When you've finished, it's an easy 20-minute drive back to the heart of **Queenstown** via SH6 and SH6A.

Macetown

Upriver from Arrowtown, and reached via either a four-wheel-drive tour with Nomad Safaris (tel: 03 442 6699; www.nomadsafaris.co.nz; daily 8am, 1.30pm) or a hiking track, is Macetown, where hundreds of miners flocked when gold was discovered in the Arrow River in 1862. The town grew rapidly, but the claims were quickly exhausted. Today Macetown is a ghost town with only three of its original buildings still standing.

Food and Drink

① THE RED TRACTOR
54 Buckingham Street, Arrowtown; tel: 03 442 0991; $$
A casual pizza restaurant housed in a beautifully restored historic building that was once the home of the local postmaster.

② ARROWTOWN BAKERY & CAFÉ
1 Ballarat Arcade, Arrowtown; tel: 03 442 1587; $
An inexpensive range of bakery items, including filled rolls, the 'Arrowtown Bakery Pie', various breads, biscuits and cakes, is made here daily from scratch.

③ GIBBSTON VALLEY WINERY RESTAURANT
SH6, Queenstown; tel: 03 442 6910; $$
Fresh local produce is used to create a menu that reflects the lifestyle of the region, with dishes such as vine-smoked venison teaming perfectly with Gibbston's own range of wines.

MILFORD SOUND

Last, but certainly not least, this tour takes you to the spectacular Milford Sound, located in Fiordland National Park. Cruise on the fiord and return via the Homer Tunnel and Te Anau to Queenstown.

Maori Masterpiece
Maori legends tell of Tu-te-raki-whanoa, the master carver who crafted the fiords with his adze, beginning in the south and working his way up the coastline to Milford Sound, his *pièce de résistance*.

DISTANCE 598km (371 miles) return
TIME One or two days
START/END Queenstown
POINTS TO NOTE

This trip can be done as a drive or with a tour operator. For car-hire information, *see p.111*. If you are driving yourself, note that it involves an arduous four- to five-hour journey each way. One option is to break this up with an overnight stay in Te Anau or Milford Sound *(see p.119)*. It is mandatory for vehicles to carry chains between May and September, and, as there are no other petrol (gas) stations, fill up your vehicle in Te Anau.

Milford Track
A hearty option is to walk in on the Milford Track, hiking a 54km (33-mile) route over three to four days, staying in huts along the way. This trail is so popular that it's fully booked for months in advance, but with some forward planning and a reasonable level of fitness, there is no better way to fully appreciate the Sound.

Milford Sound (a fiord mistakenly thought to be a sound when discovered) is set amid the rainforest of Fiordland National Park. Formed from a sunken glacial valley, it is surrounded by steep bush-clad cliffs that rise to meet the Southern Alps. It is the spectacular final destination of the **Milford Track** *(see left)* but is also accessible by road and can be reached from Queenstown in a long day. A number of tour operators, including **Real Journeys** (tel: 03 249 7416; www.realjourneys.co.nz; charge), offer day trips from **Queenstown ❶**.

TOWARDS THE SOUND

From Queenstown, leave early in the morning and travel south along the edge of **Lake Wakatipu ❷** beneath the rugged **Remarkables** mountain range through **Kingston ❸**, **Athol ❹** and **Mossburn ❺** to **Te Anau** (see ⑪① and ②) **❻**. Continue on up the **Milford Road**, through the plains of Eglinton Valley and into the **Fiordland National Park**.

Waterfalls, forested valleys, granite peaks and spectacular crystal-clear lakes clamour for attention all the way to the 1.2km (²⁄₃-mile) -long **Homer Tunnel**, a remarkable feat of engineering completed over 18 years by a team of just five men using only picks, shovels and wheelbarrows as tools; it descends dramatically to the shores of **Milford Sound ❼**. The iconic Mitre Peak rises in a ceremonial welcome, as you near the end of the 115km (71-mile) Milford Road. Refreshments are available at **Blue Duck Café**, see ⑪③, on the waterfront.

CRUISING THE SOUND

Organised tours include a cruise on the Sound, but those driving themselves can cruise, too, with **Southern Discoveries** (Milford Wharf, SH94; tel: 03 441

1137; www.southerndiscoveries.co.nz; daily, summer 9am–3.45pm, winter 9.45am–3.20pm; charge) or **Real Journeys** *(see left)*; a more energetic option is to join a kayak tour.

Highlights

During the cruise, highlights include watching Mitre Peak's three-pointed glaciated slab rise 1,692m (5,551ft) high from the Sound, marvelling at waterfalls such as Lady Bowen Falls, which tumbles 161m (528ft) from a hanging valley, and spotting bottlenose dolphins, fur seals and Fiordland crested penguins near Seal Rock.

If you visit in December, keep an eye open for the beautiful red blossoms of the southern rata, which, like the North Island's pohutukawa, is known as New Zealand's Christmas tree.

Harrison Cove

Depending on time, a recommended treat is **Harrison Cove's Underwater Observatory**, where you can peek below the top layer of fresh water to spy on deepwater species and corals. As this attraction is only accessible by boat, to get there you must book with Southern Discoveries or Real Journeys (charge).

Bowen Falls Track

Alternatively, hike the short **Bowen Falls Track**, where you're bound to meet tired but elated Milford Track hikers. For comfort, pack a waterproof jacket, since Fiordland has the highest rainfall levels in the country. Although this seldom dampens the experience, sand-

flies can, so wear long trousers and cover yourself liberally with insect repellent.

Back to Queenstown

If you are driving yourself, head back the way you came. If you travel to the Sound by organised tour, you will be back in Queenstown by 8–9pm.

Above from far left: the spectacular Milford Sound; photo opportunity en route in the Eglinton Valley.

Food and Drink

① **REDCLIFF CAFÉ**
12 Mokonui Street, Te Anau; tel: 03 249 7431; $–$$
Inspired New Zealand dishes are served in a quaint cottage.

② **OLIVE TREE CAFÉ**
52 Town Centre, Te Anau; tel: 03 249 8496; $
A good place for coffee and cake, or a light meal.

③ **BLUE DUCK CAFÉ**
SH94, Milford Sound; tel: 03 249 7931; $
Close to the waterfront, this café serves a variety of sandwiches and bakery items by day, and pub-style fare by night.

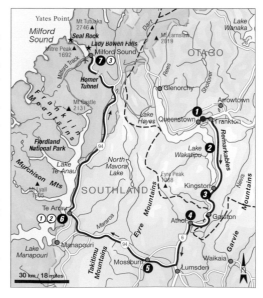

DIRECTORY

A user-friendly alphabetical listing of practical information,
plus hand-picked hotels and restaurants, clearly organised
by area, to suit all budgets and tastes.

A–Z   102
ACCOMMODATION   112
RESTAURANTS   120

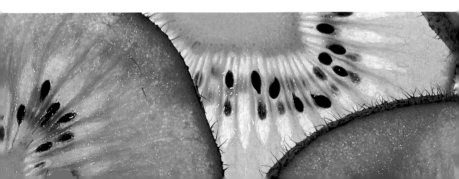

A

AGE RESTRICTIONS

The minimum age for driving in New Zealand is 15; however, you must be 21 or over (with a valid driver's licence) to hire a vehicle. The age of consent is 16. You must be 18 years or over to enter a bar and to purchase alcohol.

B

BICYCLE HIRE

New Zealand's quiet roads and stunning scenery make it ideal for cycle touring, provided you can cope with numerous hills. The South Island's Canterbury Plains do provide easy flat cycling, as does the city of Christchurch. Here bikes can be hired for NZ$15–35 a day, or NZ$200 a month for a standard touring bike in good condition. Ten-speed bikes and tandems can be hired for sightseeing in most cities, while resorts such as Queenstown and Taupo also have mountain bikes for hire. Safety helmets are compulsory, so you might want to bring your own.

Guided cycle tours ranging from six to 18 days are available; on these trips your luggage is transported by van to each lodging along the way. Backpacker transport operators such as Kiwi Experience (tel: 09 366 9830) can arrange bike hire and issue vouchers that allow you to transport your bike on their buses when you're not riding.

BUSINESS HOURS

Business hours are generally Mon–Fri 9am–5pm. Most stores and shops are open Mon–Fri 9am–5.30pm and Sat 10am–1pm. Many also stay open late (until 9pm) one night a week, usually on Thur or Fri; some stores open on Sun. In busier tourist areas and resorts, shops invariably open on Sundays and in the evenings.

Bars, pubs and taverns open Mon–Sat from 11am and close between 11pm and 2am, depending on their licence. Clubs usually open their doors at 7.30–8pm and close around 4am.

C

CRIME AND SAFETY

If you take due care, there is no reason to expect trouble in New Zealand. Take the usual sensible precautions, such as locking your car and never leaving tempting articles visible inside. Make sure camper vans are well secured. Keep valuables in the hotel safe, and don't leave valuable possessions on the beach while you swim. Any theft should be reported immediately to the police.

Drugs offences, particularly if they relate to harder drugs, are treated very seriously. Marijuana is widely available but remains illegal.

While New Zealand is a safe country, it is unwise for a lone woman to walk at night in some big-city areas, such as the 'K' Road nightlife area in Auckland. New Zealand has some

fearsome-looking motorcycle gangs on the roads, but they are unlikely to hassle tourists.

CUSTOMS AND ENTRY REQUIREMENTS

Visas and Passports

All visitors to New Zealand need a passport valid for at least three months beyond the date they intend leaving the country. Citizens of Canada, Ireland, South Africa, the US and several other countries do not require an entry visa if they intend to stay for less than three months. British passport-holders can stay visa-free for six months; Australians can stay indefinitely. To gain entry, visitors must hold fully paid onward or return tickets to a country they have permission to enter and sufficient funds to maintain themselves during their stay in New Zealand (at least NZ$1,000 per person per month).

Everyone arriving in New Zealand must complete an arrival card handed out on the aircraft.

Banned Substances

Animal products, fruit, plant material, or foodstuffs that could contain plant or animal pests and diseases are banned. Heavy fines are imposed on people caught carrying these. Leave all food on the aircraft, or place in the bins provided on the approach to the immigration area.

Drugs, including marijuana and cocaine, are illegal in New Zealand; penalties for possession are heavy and risk affecting your visa status.

Duty on Imported Goods

Goods up to a total combined value of NZ$700 are free of duty and tax, but goods in excess of this may attract both. If you are over 17 you may also take the following into New Zealand free of duty and tax: 200 cigarettes or 250 grams of tobacco or 50 cigars (or a mixture of all three not weighing more than 250 grams); 4.5 litres of wine (equivalent to six standard 750-ml wine bottles) or 4.5 litres of beer and three 1,125-ml bottles of spirits or liqueur. There is no restriction on the import or export of foreign or local currency.

Visitors to New Zealand may purchase duty-free goods, which are not subject to local taxes, from airport duty-free shops upon arrival and departure. Duty-free stores in central Auckland, Wellington and Christchurch can deliver purchases to aircraft departure lounges.

E

ELECTRICITY

230V/50Hz AC is standard. Most hotels have sockets for 110V AC electric razors. The country uses Australasian/Pacific-model plugs with three flat pins.

EMBASSIES AND CONSULATES

The following is a list of the main consular offices in New Zealand:

Australia: 72–6 Hobson Street, Thorndon, Wellington; tel: 04 473 6411; www.australia.org.nz.
Canada: 125 The Terrace, Wellington (PO Box 8047), Wellington; tel: 04 473 9577; www.wellington.gc.ca.
Ireland: Level 7, Citigroup Building, 23 Customs Street East, Auckland; tel: 09 977 2252; www.ireland.co.nz.
UK: 44 Hill Street, Wellington (PO Box 1812), Wellington 6140; tel: 04 924 2888; www.britain.org.nz.
US: 29 Fitzherbert Terrace, Thorndon (PO Box 1190), Wellington; tel: 04 462 6000; http://newzealand.usembassy.gov.

EMERGENCIES

Dial 111 for emergency calls to police, fire or ambulance services. Emergency numbers for doctors, dentists, hospitals and local authorities are given in the front of local telephone directories and posted in telephone boxes. Police control call-outs for search-and-rescue services in the bush.

Fire Hazards

Fire poses a constant threat to New Zealand's natural beauty. In summer, scrub and grass are tinder-dry, and the slightest spark can start a blaze. Do not throw matches or cigarettes from car windows, and don't light fires in restricted areas. Beach barbecues are tolerated as long as you remain a safe distance from trees, but be sure to shelter the fire well from sea breezes – a chance cinder can set a whole bush-bound coast alight. Always extinguish a fire carefully by dousing

it with water or covering it with earth. Glass can concentrate the sun's rays and start fires, so store empty bottles in the shade and take them with you when you leave.

G

GAY AND LESBIAN TRAVELLERS

New Zealand is not generally a homophobic country, although prejudice may persist in smaller towns. The country has a history of enlightened laws relating to human rights. Homosexuality ceased to be categorised as a criminal offence in 1986, and the age of consent was set at 16 (the same as for heterosexuals).

There are lots of facilities and activities in New Zealand catering for gay, lesbian and bisexual travellers, including Gay Ski Week in Queenstown and the Great Party weekend in Wellington. For further information, contact Gay Tourism New Zealand (www.gaytravel.co.nz).

GUIDES AND TOURS

A wide choice of escorted package tours is available. These include fly/drive arrangements (with or without accommodation), camper or motorhome hire, fully escorted coach holidays (North Island, South Island, or both), escorted budget coach holidays, farm holidays, trekking holidays and ski packages.

A scenic flight tour is recommended

at any of the following destinations: Rotorua, Mount Cook, the Fox and Franz Josef glaciers, Queenstown and Milford Sound. Alpine flights use special planes with retractable skis for landing on snow and ice.

HEALTH CARE

Both public and private health services are of a high standard in New Zealand. Hotels and motels usually have a doctor on call, and doctors are listed separately at the front of telephone directories. Medical services are not free, except as a result of an accident, so you are strongly advised to arrange health insurance in advance. In the case of an accident, all visitors are entitled to compensation, covering expenses such as doctor's fees and hospitalisation. New Zealand has reciprocal health agreements with Australia and the UK, but not with any other countries.

Insects and Venomous Creatures

You don't have to worry about venomous creepy-crawlies in New Zealand. The only venomous spider, the katipo, is rare and retiring, and there are no snakes. However, there is a flying pest that delivers a painful, itchy bite: the gnat-sized sandfly. It is prevalent on the West Coast of the South Island, so ensure you carry insect repellent if travelling in this area. The European wasp, with its yellow-and-black-striped abdomen, has colonised New Zealand and become a problem in some bush areas. Hikers should carry antihistamine medication as a precaution.

Sunburn

Guard against sunburn every day in the summer (even when there is cloud cover) and in alpine areas year-round, by using a factor 30 sunscreen lotion.

Pharmacies

Chemists (pharmacies) usually open 9am–5.30pm Mon–Fri, as well as on Sat morning. The addresses and phone numbers of emergency chemists (for after-hours service) are posted on the doors of all pharmacies.

Drinking Water

New Zealand has an excellent public water supply. Tap water is safe to drink.

HOLIDAYS

The major public holidays are:
1 and 2 Jan: New Year
6 Feb: Waitangi Day
Mar/Apr: Good Friday, Easter Monday
25 Apr: Anzac Day
June: Queen's Birthday (first Mon)
Oct: Labour Day (fourth Mon)
25/26 Dec: Christmas, Boxing Day

LAUNDRY/DRY CLEANING

The majority of motels and some hotels have self-service laundry facilities. Large hotels provide laundry

Above from far left: red-blossoming pohutukawa tree on the Coromandel Peninsula; the New Zealand bush.

Extra Holidays
When Christmas, Boxing Day or New Year's Day falls on a Saturday or Sunday, the public holiday is observed on the following Monday. Also, each province holds a holiday on its own anniversary. These range through the year and can vary, so it's worth checking with an authority such as Tourism New Zealand (www.new zealand.com) before you depart.

Above from left:
Aoraki Mount
Cook; Zorbing.

and dry-cleaning services. At local dry cleaners your clothing will usually be returned to you in 48 hours, although you can generally pay more for a speedier service.

M

MAPS

Tourist offices and car-hire companies distribute free maps. The New Zealand Automobile Association also produces regional maps and excellent district maps. Alternatively, Hema Maps, Wises Maps and Kiwi Maps are also well produced and widely available throughout the country.

MEDIA

Newspapers and Magazines

Mass-circulation daily newspapers are produced in New Zealand's main population centres. *The Herald* in Auckland is the North Island's largest circulation paper, while *The Press* in Christchurch is the South Island's largest. There are also local daily papers published in provincial centres and most towns. International papers and magazines can be found in large bookstores in the main cities.

The Listener, a weekly news magazine, publishes a television and radio guide as well as articles on the arts and social issues. *Metro* and *North and South* current affairs magazines provide lively, informative and topical features. International magazines are widely available.

Television

Sky television (featuring BBC News and CNN) is widely available, otherwise television consists of ten free commercial channels as well as a number of regional television stations. Commercials proliferate on channels 1–3, along with many overseas-made repeats and some local content.

Radio

National Radio is the best station for news, current events and quality programming; numerous other stations cater to all tastes. The BBC World Service is easy to tune into throughout the country, and presents news and current events to a high standard, albeit from a distant part of the planet.

MONEY

Currency

New Zealand has a decimal currency system, with one dollar made up of 100 cents. Coins come in denominations of 10¢, 20¢, 50¢, NZ$1 and NZ$2. Notes come in NZ$5, NZ$10, NZ$20, NZ$50 and NZ$100 denominations.

Banking Hours

These are usually 9am–4.30pm Mon–Fri. Some branches open on Sat until 12.30pm.

Credit Cards

Internationally recognised credit cards are widely accepted, and major currencies such as US dollars, UK pounds and Australian dollars can be readily changed at banks.

International credit cards encoded with a PIN may be used to withdraw cash from automatic teller machines (ATMs), which are widely available in main shopping centres and suburban malls. Check with your bank before departure to ensure this facility is available to you, and whether you will be charged for every withdrawal.

NB: Note that 'Smart Cards', which often have no magnetic strip, are not universally accepted in New Zealand, so contact your card provider for further information prior to your trip.

Traveller's Cheques

Traveller's cheques can also be cashed at banks, bigger hotels and tourist-orientated shops.

Goods and Service Tax

A 12.5 percent Goods and Service Tax (GST), generally included in the quoted price (except with trade goods), is slapped onto virtually everything.

P

POLICE

New Zealand police are approachable and helpful, although note that some carry taser guns.

See also Emergencies, p.104.

POST OFFICES

Main post offices (Post Shops) sell stationery as well as offering postal and banking services. In rural areas the general store doubles as the Post Shop.

It costs NZ$1.80 to send postcards to anywhere in the world. International airmail envelopes cost NZ$1.80 to Australia and NZ$2.30 to the rest of the world. Domestic mail is divided into first- (FastPost) and second-class (Standard).

R

RELIGION

New Zealand has no state Church, but Christianity is the dominant religion. Protestants outnumber Catholics. The daily papers give details of addresses and times of services.

S

SMOKING

Smoking is not permitted in any restaurants, bars or public buildings in New Zealand.

T

TELEPHONES

Landlines and Public (Pay) Phones

Calls that are made on private phones are vastly cheaper than those made on public (pay) phones. Local calls from private phones are free to other landlines.

Coin-operated phones are rare in New Zealand, although a few remain at airports and railway stations. Card-operated public phones with trunk

Population
New Zealand has 4 million people, mostly of British descent, with the largest minority (about 12 percent) being Maori of Polynesian origin. New Zealanders are sometimes called 'Kiwis' after the flightless bird that is the country's unofficial national symbol (not after the small furry fruit that also shares the Kiwi name!) You may also hear the term *Pakeha*, which is the Maori term for Europeans.

(toll) and international direct dialling (IDD) options are located throughout the country.

Phone cards are readily available from post offices, supermarkets and petrol stations; they come in denominations of NZ$5, NZ$10, NZ$20 and NZ$50.

Dialling Codes

The country code for New Zealand is 64. To call abroad, first dial the international access code, 00, then the country code.

Mobile (Cell) Phones

Cell phones operate on GSM and 3G networks, and are provided by a variety of operators including Vodafone (www.vodafone.com) and Telecom (www.telecom.co.nz). Mobile phone hire, including prepay options, is readily available. It is far cheaper to make calls using a hired mobile or to purchase a local SIM card for your own mobile (as long as it has an international roaming facility) as local call rates will apply.

TIME

New Zealand is one of the first places in the world to see the new day, 12 hours ahead of GMT (Greenwich Mean Time). In summer New Zealand uses 'daylight saving', with clocks put forward one hour to GMT+13. Daylight saving begins on the last Sunday in September and ends on the first Sunday of the following April, when clocks are put back to GMT+12.

TIPPING

Tipping is uncommon in New Zealand; however, restaurant, hospitality and tourism staff will appreciate a tip if their service has been good. Taxi drivers do not expect tips, and service charges are not added to hotel or restaurant bills.

TOILETS

Toilets for public use are found in hotel lobbies, shopping centres, large stores, restaurants, museums, cinemas and pubs. Most towns provide public 'rest rooms'; they are also located in most picnic spots along main roads and at the most popular beaches.

TOURIST INFORMATION

Within New Zealand

New Zealand has an established network of visitor information centres known as i-SITES.

Outside New Zealand

Tourism New Zealand (www.newzealand.com) maintains marketing and information offices in the following countries:

Australia: Level 8, 35 Pitt Street, Sydney, NSW 2000; tel: 02 9247 5222.
UK: New Zealand House, 80 Haymarket, London SW1Y 4TQ; tel: 020 7930 8422.
US: Suite 300, 501 Santa Monica Boulevard, Santa Monica, CA 90401; tel: 866 639 9325.

TRANSPORT

Getting to New Zealand

From Australia: Frequent direct flights operated by Air New Zealand and Qantas link Sydney and Auckland each day. Recent developments have seen flight frequency increase, with more services flown by B737 aircraft. These days, Australian airlines view New Zealand as virtually a domestic destination. The same view applies vice versa – though obviously you need appropriate documents to travel between the two countries. Qantas and Air New Zealand offer direct flights to Auckland from major Australian cities. Direct flights also operate between Christchurch and Wellington from Brisbane, Melbourne and Sydney. Freedom Air, an Air New Zealand subsidiary, also links centres on each side of the Tasman Sea.

From North America: Auckland is linked with Los Angeles by direct flights, taking less than 13 hours, on average. Several connections a day run from Auckland to Wellington or Christchurch. New Zealand can also be reached with an additional one or two stops in the Pacific. It can be reached from New York City in just two stops and from San Francisco in one stop.

From the UK: Regular weekly flights operate by airlines including Air New Zealand, Qantas and various Asian carriers from London to New Zealand with one, two or three stops en route. Since the journey takes at least 24 hours, the cheapest ticket may not be the best deal – it may involve more than one airline and two or more stops, typically requiring you to change aircraft (and possibly airlines) in Singapore, Hong Kong, Sydney or Los Angeles.

Airports

Auckland (AKL) International is 22km (13½ miles) south of the city centre. Transfer to the city by taxi or bus (30–45 mins).
Christchurch (CHC) International is 10km (6 miles) northwest of the city centre. Transfer to the city by taxi or bus (25 mins).
Wellington (WLG) International is 8km (5 miles) southeast of the city centre. Transfer to the city by taxi or bus (15 mins).

Long-haul international flights generally land in Auckland. Trans-Tasman flights from Australia also serve Wellington, Auckland and Christchurch, with additional direct air links between Australia and smaller centres such as Queenstown, Hamilton, Dunedin and Palmerston North.

Domestic Flights

Air New Zealand is the primary domestic carrier, with Qantas and Pacific Blue competing on main trunk routes. A number of smaller companies serve provincial towns. There are frequent flights from the main centres, provincial towns and resort areas.

Above from far left: hiking in Marlborough wine country; Mitre Peak, Fiordland.

City Buses/Trains

Local **buses** run according to a published timetable. Fares are calculated according to the number of 'sections' travelled. Some city shuttle buses have 'honesty boxes', into which you drop the required amount. Wellington has electric trains that travel to the northern suburbs and Auckland runs trains serving suburbs to the south and west.

Coach Services

Coaches provide countryside service. Many are air-conditioned although all are heated in winter. The main national coach providers are InterCity (www.intercity.co.nz; www.travelpass.co.nz) and Naked Bus (www.nakedbus.co.nz). Budget-priced backpacker coaches such as Kiwi Experience (www.kiwiexperience.com) and Magic Bus (www.magicbus.co.nz) also cover major routes.

A number of coach companies offer **passes** along the routes they operate, either with unlimited stops along a fixed line or a certain number of travel days within a set time frame. Some passes include one ferry and one train journey. Discounts of up to 15 percent are offered to seniors, students, backpackers and children. Earlybird fares starting from $1 are available online.

Trains

New Zealand offers three scenic long-distance rail services. For full details, contact Tranz Scenic, tel: 04 495 0775; www.tranzscenic.co.nz. Here is a rundown of one-way adult fares:

Overlander (Auckland–Wellington), from NZ$49.

TranzCoastal (Christchurch–Picton), from NZ$39.

TranzAlpine (Christchurch–Greymouth), from NZ$39.

Scenic rail passes are also available; prices for adults begin at NZ$301.

Ferries

The North and South Islands are linked by both passenger and vehicular ferries (www.interislander.co.nz; www.bluebridge.co.nz), which depart frequently. Stewart Island and Great Barrier Island are also connected by ferry, with less frequent daily departures.

Driving

Road Conditions: roads are generally good, and light traffic in remoter parts of the country makes driving a pleasure, although roads can be tortuously windy. Auckland often has traffic jams outside of peak hours due to the ongoing and extensive upgrading of its road infrastructure.

Rules and Regulations: provided you hold a valid overseas driver's licence or an international driving permit, you can drive in New Zealand for up to one year before you are required to apply for a New Zealand licence. You must be able to prove you hold a valid overseas licence and drive only those types of vehicles for which you were licensed in your country of origin. Carry your licence or permit with you whenever you are driving.

Traffic keeps to the left. Drivers must yield (give way) to every vehicle approaching or crossing from their

right. Seat belts are compulsory for all passengers. Helmets are compulsory for motorcyclists and sidecar passengers. Maximum speed limits are 50kmh (30mph) in built-up areas unless otherwise indicated, 100kmh (60mph) on open roads. Road hazards include slips, rock falls, possums, quail, flocks of sheep and herds of cows, so go carefully. If you should encounter animals on the road, take your time and edge through them, or get someone to walk ahead to clear a path for the vehicle.

Fuel Costs: fuel is generally cheaper in cities than it is in country areas.

Roadside Assistance: the New Zealand Automobile Association offers free services and privileges to members of accredited overseas motoring organisations. It also handles vehicle insurance. Through the Association you can make reservations for accommodation and the inter-island ferry. See its website, www.nzaa.co.nz, or contact one of the following offices: Auckland: 99 Albert Street, tel: 09 377 4660; Wellington: 342–52 Lambton Quay, tel: 04 931 9999; Christchurch: 210 Hereford Street, tel: 03 964 3650.

Car Hire: to rent a car you will need an approved national or international driving licence. The minimum age is 21, and drivers under 25 sometimes have to pay more for insurance. Major international firms such as Avis, Hertz and Budget have offices in New Zealand, but local firms such as Apex can often offer cheaper deals. Hire cars range from NZ$40–200 per day, with rates fluctuating seasonally and varying according to the length of rental. Camper vans cost from NZ$90 or less in low season to NZ$375 for a six-berth in high season.

Note, however, that even if you take out a collision-damage waiver, you can still end up paying for the first NZ$500 or NZ$1,000 of any damage to your hire vehicle – whether you are responsible for the accident or not. However, several firms offer extra insurance to reduce your exposure to this insidious charge.

Chauffeur-driven vehicles are available for short or long trips. Taxi companies also provide the services of experienced driver-guides. Rates usually include basic mileage plus the driver's living expenses and vary according to the number of passengers.

VACCINATIONS

No vaccination certificates are needed for entry into New Zealand. However, if within three weeks of your arrival you develop any sickness such as a skin rash, fever and chills, diarrhoea or vomiting, you should consult a doctor *(see Health Care, p.105)*.

VISAS AND PASSPORTS

See Customs and Entry Requirements, p.103.

Accommodation in New Zealand ranges from five-star city hotels and luxury country lodges to low-cost backpacker hostels. The country's top hotels – all the well-known chains are represented – are comparable to those anywhere in the world. Serviced apartments and all-suite hotels start from about NZ$700 a week. Luxury lodges, usually compact and distinctive mansions or custom-designed villas of exceptional quality, offer world-class service and sublime surroundings at NZ$400–1,000 a night. Backpackers are served by more than 250 hostels, some in settings that are just as splendid as those enjoyed by more expensive establishments; rates start at NZ$15–20 per person for a shared room.

Auckland Central

City Life Auckland

171 Queen Street; tel: 09 379 9222; www.heritagehotels.co.nz; $$$–$$$$
Located in the heart of the CBD, City Life Auckland offers a range of rooms from suites to apartments, all with an en-suite bathroom, Sky (cable) TV, broadband internet connection and minibar. Facilities here include an indoor heated lap pool, gymnasium, guest laundry, restaurant, bar and busi-

Price guide for a double room with bathroom for one night:

$$$$$	over NZ$350
$$$$	NZ$250–350
$$$	NZ$150–250
$$	NZ$100–150
$	below NZ$100

ness services centre. Room service is available 24 hours and Wi-fi internet connections can be found in all public places within the hotel.

Heritage Auckland

35 Hobson Street; tel: 09 379 8553; www.heritagehotels.co.nz; $$$–$$$$
A top-class hotel with friendly staff in a mid-city Auckland location near the Skycity casino and within walking distance of the Viaduct Harbour and the Aotea Centre. The building was once an old department store, and it has been beautifully restored. Health club, heated outdoor swimming pool and fine dining restaurant.

President Hotel

27–35 Victoria Street West; tel: 09 303 1333; www.president hotel.co.nz; $$$
Part of the Best Western Group, the President Hotel is well located and offers excellent value, especially for families or larger groups travelling together. Rooms range from standard studios through to two-bedroom suites with a separate lounge; all are non-smoking and air-conditioned. Limited secure car parking is available (pre-booking is essential) and facilities include a guest laundry, gym, internet room and wireless access, licensed restaurant, and dry-cleaning service.

Skycity Hotel and Skycity Grand Hotel

Corner of Victoria and Federal streets; tel: 09 363 6000; www.skycity.co.nz; $$$–$$$$$

The Skycity Hotel is located within the Skycity casino and theatre complex, with its 18 bars, cafés and restaurants and the Sky Tower. The Grand is a more upmarket, luxurious oasis that includes the acclaimed 'Dine by Peter Gordon' restaurant *(see p.120)*, plus gym, pool and spa. The buildings face each other in the heart of downtown Auckland.

Greater Auckland Region

Gulf Harbour Lodge

164 Harbour Village Drive, Whangaparaoa Peninsula; tel: 09 428 1118; www.gulfharbourlodge.com; $$$–$$$$$

On Hauraki Gulf, one hour's drive north of the city, this canalside lodge has a distinctly Mediterranean feel. Country Club facilities include golf course, tennis and squash courts, heated pool and gymnasium. Daily ferry operates to Auckland's city centre.

Parnell City Lodge

2 St Stephens Avenue, Parnell; tel: 09 377 1463; www.parnellcity lodge.co.nz; $$–$$$

Choose between elegant Edwardian rooms and modern apartments near the shops in Parnell, five minutes from downtown Auckland. Twenty-one stylish units available, all with off-street parking right outside. Most units have self-contained kitchens.

Peace and Plenty Inn

6 Flagstaff Terrace, Devonport; tel: 09 445 2925; www.peaceand plenty.co.nz; $$$–$$$$

Set in the lovely, historic harbourside village of Devonport, Peace and Plenty is only a 10-minute ferry ride to Auckland's city centre. Five spacious guest suites, each providing king- and queen-sized beds and high-quality bed linens, and delights from the colonial era including deep claw-foot baths, cast-iron fireplaces and polished floors. Gourmet breakfast is served in a sunny breakfast room or alfresco overlooking the tropical garden of palms, frangipani and hibiscus blooms.

Waitakere Estate

573 Scenic Drive, Waitakere Ranges; tel: 09 814 9622; www.waitakere estate.co.nz; $$$–$$$$$

A private paradise surrounded by rainforest, perched 240m (800ft) above sea level. The original builder of the hotel, which started life as a family home, had to cut his way through bush to reach the spot where it now stands. The 17 suites have modern facilities, a library and kauri lounge. Gorgeous views over Auckland and the Hauraki Gulf.

Northland

Abel Tasman Lodge

Corner Marsden and Bayview Roads; tel: 09 402 7521; www.abeltasmanlodge.co.nz; $–$$$

Twenty-five self-contained apartment-style units featuring full kitchen and bathroom facilities; most apartments provide sea views. Spa pools (one private spa located indoors, the second in a garden setting). Guest laundry, Sky (cable) TV, and tour desk with free booking service.

Bream Bay Motel

67 Bream Bay Drive, Ruakaka; tel:
09 432 7166; www.breambay
motel.co.nz; $–$$$

Self-contained one- and two-bed-
room units set right on a popular surf
beach. Upstairs units provide stunning
views of Bream Bay. The motel is
located 1½ hours' drive north of
Auckland, half an hour south of
Whangarei, and 1½ hours south of
Paihia and the Bay of Islands.

Edgewater Palms Apartments

8–10 Marsden Road, Paihia; tel
09 402 0090; www.edgewater
apartments.co.nz; $$$$$

Upmarket self-contained apartments
with an outdoor saltwater pool and spa
set in an attractive waterfront location
close to the vibrant wharf. All apart-
ments feature sea views.

Coromandel Peninsula

Admiralty Lodge Motel

69–71 Buffalo Beach Road, Whitianga;
tel: 07 866 0181; $$$–$$$$

Nicely appointed beach-front apart-
ments, all with views of Buffalo Beach
and Mercury Bay. Off-street parking,
heated swimming pool, and compli-
mentary newspapers daily.

Price guide for a double room with bathroom for one night:	
$$$$$	over NZ$350
$$$$	NZ$250–350
$$$	NZ$150–250
$$	NZ$100–150
$	below NZ$100

Rotorua

Acapulco Motel

Corner Malfroy Road and Eason
Street; tel: 07 347 9569;
www.acapulcomotel.net.nz; $

In a quiet location near the city centre,
this good-value motel with friendly
hosts has 15 rooms. a thermally heated
pool and a mineral spa.

Millennium Rotorua

Corner of Eruera and Hinemaru
streets; tel: 07 347 1234; www.
millenniumrotorua.co.nz; $$$–$$$$$

Deluxe hotel in the middle of town.
Ask for a room overlooking the Poly-
nesian Pools and Lake Rotorua, as
there are great views from the balcony.
Facilities include a gym and pool.

Solitaire Lodge

Ronald Road, Lake Tarawera; tel: 07
362 8208; www.solitairelodge.co.nz;
$$$$$

Nestled in bushland on a private penin-
sula 25 minutes from Rotorua, this
deluxe lodge with ten suites has great
views of the lake and Mount Tarawera.

Sudima Hotel

1000 Eurera Street; tel: 07 348 1174;
www.sudimahotels.com; $–$$$

Just opposite the Polynesian Spa, this
hotel has superb views of the lake and
thermal areas. There's a restaurant, bar
and private thermal spa pools. Within
walking distance of Rotorua centre.

Wylie Court Motor Lodge

345 Fenton Street; tel: 07 347 7879;
www.wyliecourt.co.nz; $$–$$$

Standard and executive suites, plus outdoor heated swimming pools set in one hectare (2 acres) of gardens. Restaurant open daily. Wheelchair access. 36 units.

Taupo

Gables Motor Lodge

130 Lake Terrace; tel: 07 378 8030; www.gablesmotorlodge.co.nz; $$

Right opposite Lake Taupo's main swimming beach. Twelve self-contained one-bedroom units, each with a private spa pool.

Huka Lodge

271 Huka Falls Road; tel: 07 378 5791; www.hukalodge.co.nz; $$$$$+

Regularly rated as one of the best hotels in the world, the 1920s Huka Lodge is the height of understated luxury, around an hour's drive from Rotorua. It is set within extensive grounds above the Huka Falls, with 20 suites dotted among trees by the Waikato River. Fine restaurant. Wheelchair access.

Suncourt Hotel

14 Northcroft Street; tel: 07 378 8265; www.suncourt.co.nz; $–$$$

This 52-room complex offers a range of accommodation from studio units to two-bedroom units, 40 of which provide uninterrupted views of Lake Taupo and the mountains of Tongariro National Park.

Wellington

Duxton Hotel Wellington

170 Wakefield Street; tel: 04 473 3900; www.duxtonhotels.com; $$–$$$$

Located in the heart of the CBD, close to the waterfront, the Duxton has 192 tastefully appointed rooms. Its award-winning Grill Restaurant serves a fusion of national and international cuisine.

Intercontinental Wellington

2 Grey Street; tel: 04 472 2722; www.intercontinental.com/wellington; $$$$–$$$$$

Right on the waterfront, this hotel has a restaurant, bars and a fitness centre with heated pool and sauna.

Stillwater Lodge

34 Mana Esplanade, Paremata; tel: 04 233 6628; www.stillwaterlodge.co.nz; $

Bargain basement backpackers' beach paradise, around 20 minutes north of Wellington on the beachfront.

Tinakori Lodge Bed and Breakfast

182 Tinakori Road; tel: 04 939 3478; www.tinakorilodge.co.nz; $–$$

This appealing place is handy for rail links, the Botanic Garden and restaurants in the historic Thorndon area. Quality facilities, restful atmosphere and scrumptious breakfast buffet, too.

The Wairarapa

Parehua Country Estate

New York Street, Martinborough; tel: 06 306 8405; www.parehua.co.nz; $$$$$

Twenty-eight contemporary villas and cottages are located in landscaped grounds at the edge of this popular wine region of Wairarapa.

Camping

Since much of New Zealand's appeal lies out of doors, camping is a great way to see the country. Many people rent a self-contained motor-home or a camper van; most include heating, toilets, fridges and cookers. Holiday Parks (motor camps) near main resorts provide electricity and toilet, kitchen and laundry facilities. Some offer cabins; for these you provide your own bedding, linen and cutlery. Prices vary according to standards and season. Advance reservations are necessary during January, when New Zealanders are on holiday. New Zealand also has a number of Department of Conservation (DOC) sites with basic facilities; visitors are welcome to park overnight for a small fee.

'Freedom camping' in lay-bys or rest areas in non-self-contained vehicles (ie without toilets) is not advised.

Peppers Martinborough Hotel

The Square; tel: 06 306 9350; www.
peppers.co.nz/Martinborough; $$$$$

Around 75 minutes' drive east of
Wellington, this elegant colonial
hotel was established in 1882 as a
stopping point for prosperous travellers between the area's isolated
sheep stations. It's now a gorgeous
retreat – beautifully styled and elegant – with a good restaurant that
serves European cuisine. Has wireless internet access and all mod cons.
Close to several golf courses.

Harbour View Motel

30 Waikawa Road, Picton; tel: 03
573ʹ6259; www.harbourviewpicton.
co.nz; $$–$$$

As the name suggests, every room has
a full lookout on to the waterfront, plus
a private balcony and fully equipped
kitchen. A short stroll leads to the
water's edge and the heart of Picton.
Friendly Kiwi hosts.

Sennen House

9 Oxford Street, Picton; tel: 03 573
5216; www.sennenhouse.co.nz;
$$$$–$$$$$

This bed-and-breakfast and self-
catering apartment accommodation is
set inside an historic Picton manor
that has been sympathetically restored.
Each apartment or suite has its own
entrance, en-suite bathroom, satellite
television and comfortable beds with
pure cotton percale linen. A generous
daily breakfast hamper is included in
the tariff.

Dylans Country Cottages

268 Postmans Road; tel: 03 319
5473; www.lavenderfarm.co.nz; $$

Peaceful, private self-contained country
cottages nestled on a fragrant lavender
farm at the foot of Mount Fyffe.
Choice of indoor spa bath or secluded
outdoor courtyard bath – perfect for
stargazing. Breakfast is included in the
tariff. To avoid disappointment book in
advance as this is an extremely pop-
ular place to stay.

Hapuku Lodge and Tree Houses

Station Road; tel: 03 319 6559;
www.hapukulodge.com; $$$–$$$$$

A short rural stroll from the seafront,
this luxury lodge features five distinctive designer treehouses, plus a number
of well-appointed lodge rooms. It is set
amid landscaped gardens and is surrounded by a deer farm.

White Morph Motor Inn

92 The Esplanade; tel: 03 319 5014;
www.whitemorph.co.nz; $$$$

Superbly located in a quiet spot on
the waterfront, 20m (66ft) from the
water's edge. The apartments include
luxury hydrotherapy spa studios with
balconies and sea views, garden studios
and spa apartments. Recommended.

Cargill's Hotel

678 George Street, Dunedin; tel: 03
477 7983; www.cargills.co.nz; $$

This centrally-located hotel has spa-
cious, immaculate and quiet rooms. The

Atrium Restaurant serves breakfast and dinner, and the Neesham Lounge Bar opens onto a pretty courtyard.

Hulmes Court Bed and Breakfast

52 Tennyson Street, Dunedin; tel: 0800 448 563; www.hulmes.co.nz; $$–$$$

Clean and comfortable rooms are offered in this beautiful 1860s Victorian mansion located in the heart of the city. Each guest room has different decor and there is off-street parking for all guests.

Larnach Lodge

145 Camp Road, Otago Peninsula; tel: 03 476 1616; www.larnach castle.co.nz; $$$–$$$$

Situated at Larnach Castle, the guest rooms at Larnach Lodge feature individual period-styled bedrooms with ensuite bathrooms, and breathtaking ocean views. Cheaper stable-stay rooms with shared bathroom facilities are also available. Great if you enjoy peace and quiet instead of bustling city streets.

Albergo Lodge

80 Rippingdale Road; tel: 03 315 7428; www.albergohanmer.com; $$–$$$$$

Relaxation and rejuvenation are paramount at the hot springs resort town of Hanmer, and nowhere is it so easily achieved than at Albergo Lodge. Set on 0.8 hectares (2 acres) of landscaped alpine gardens and lawns, the luxury suites all have double glazing, under-floor heating, and offer alpine views from every window. Hanmer's thermal pools, boutiques, restaurants and cafés are a 10-minute walk away.

The Hermitage Hotel

Terrace Road, Aoraki Mount Cook Village; tel: 03 435 1809; www. hermitage.co.nz; $$$–$$$$$

The Hermitage alpine resort comprises the main Hermitage Hotel, plus the Hermitage Motels and Chalets, offering 214 rooms with views of Aoraki Mount Cook and the Southern Alps through enormous picture windows. Facilities include a sauna, babysitting service and laundry. The hotel also houses the Panorama restaurant *(see p.85)*, where world-class cuisine is created using local produce.

Bealey Hotel

SH73, Arthur's Pass; tel: 03 318 9277; www.bealeyhotel.co.nz; $–$$

Located some 12km (8 miles) east of Arthur's Pass, this modern hotel in an historic spot *(see p.87)* offers a small number of motel-style units with basic facilities and lodge rooms, all with spectacular river and mountain views.

Above from far left: lakeside view; enjoy Larnach Castle Garden from the Larnach Lodge; stylish bedroom with sea views.

Price guide for a double room with bathroom for one night:	
$$$$$	over NZ$350
$$$$	NZ$250–350
$$$	NZ$150–250
$$	NZ$100–150
$	below NZ$100

Queenstown

Copthorne Lakefront Resort

Corner of Adelaide and Frankton roads; tel: 03 442 8123; www.copthornelakefront.co.nz; $$$–$$$$$

Four-star accommodation with 241 cosy rooms, many with views of the lake and mountains. Not in the centre of Queenstown but within walking distance of the main shopping area. Shuttle service available.

The Millennium

Corner of Frankton Road and Stanley Street; tel: 03 441 8888; www.millen niumhotels.co.nz; $$$–$$$$$

This large centrally located top-class hotel lacks lake views but has excellent facilities, including a gymnasium, sauna and spa. Wheelchair access.

Nugget Point Boutique Hotel

146 Arthur's Point Road; tel: 03 441 0288; www.distinctionqueenstown. co.nz; $$$$$

An award-winning boutique property just 10 minutes' drive from Queenstown. The suites are impeccably furnished, with the more expensive ones featuring stunning views of the Shotover River and Coronet Peak.

YHA Queenstown Lakefront

88–90 Lake Esplanade; tel: 03 442 8413; www.yha.co.nz; $

Right on the waterfront among luxury hotels, there is no other accommodation in Queenstown that offers such good value for money. A choice of single or shared rooms is available here.

Arrowtown

Millbrook Resort

Malaghans Road; tel: 03 441 7000; www.millbrook.co.nz; $$$$$

Located between Queenstown and Arrowtown, this large resort provides luxurious modern accommodation in restored historic buildings with Alpine views. Among the attractions are an 18-hole golf course, an award-winning restaurant, tennis courts, two swimming pools and a spa.

Settlers Cottage Motel

22 Hertford Street; tel: 03 442 1734; www.settlerscottagemotel.co.nz; $$

A boutique motel in a quiet location close to Arrowtown's main street ,with cosy, gold-rush-themed studios and one- and two-bed apartments.

Hokitika

Fitzherbert Court

191 Fitzherbert Street; tel: 03 755 5342; www.fitzherbertcourt.co.nz; $–$$

Located close to town, these 12 ground-floor units offer full kitchen facilities, Sky (cable) TV, broadband, spa baths in six units, a children's playground and guest laundry.

Shining Star Chalets & Accommodation

16 Richards Drive; tel: 03 755 8921; www.shiningstar.co.nz; $–$$

Set among gardens right on the beach and with an exclusive beach walkway, these chalets are ideal for families and couples wanting space and peaceful surroundings. Chalets are well appointed

and facilities include a sauna, spa pool, BBQ area, children's playground, movie hire and wireless broadband.

58 On Cron Motel

58 Cron Street; tel: 03 752 0627; www.58oncron.co.nz; $$–$$$$

Brand-new, modern apartment-style motel offering 16 ground-floor units. Perfectly positioned directly opposite glacier hot pools. Rooms have super-sized beds, quality bed linen and spa baths. Guest laundry, BBQ, tour desk, Sky (cable) TV and Wi-fi internet.

Holly Homestead Bed and Breakfast

SH6, Franz Josef Glacier; tel: 03 752 0299; www.hollyhomestead.co.nz; $$$–$$$$$

Set inside a gracious old homestead, this popular place offers comfortable upmarket rooms, a cosy guest lounge and alpine views. The hosts can provide helpful advice on local activities.

Greymouth

Gables Motor Lodge

84 High Street; tel: 03 768 9991; www.gablesmotorlodge.com; $–$$$

Luxury self-contained studio, one-bedroom and two-bedroom suites, some with spa baths. Located opposite Greymouth's aquatic centre and close to shops, restaurants and cafés.

Fox Glacier

Rainforest Motel

15 Cook Flat Road, Fox Glacier; tel: 03 751 0140; www.rainforestmotel.co.nz; $–$$$$

Perfect for families, this spacious and clean motel comprises studios and one- and (large) two-bedroom units, all with kitchens, en-suite bathrooms and views of the Southern Alps and local rainforest. Two minutes' walk from town, it's the pick of the bunch on Cook Flat Road.

Te Anau

Te Anau Hotel and Villas

64 Lakefront Drive; tel: 03 249 9700; www.distinctionteanau.co.nz; $$$–$$$$$

Situated directly on the lakefront, this large hotel has a range of spacious rooms and suites, all furnished in the modern style and many with commanding views of the lake. Facilities include a restaurant/bar, spa pool and sauna. A good stop en route to/from Milford Sound.

Milford Sound

Milford Sound Lodge

SH94; tel: 03 249 8071; www.milfordlodge.com; $–$$$$

Accommodation ranges from camp sites and dorm rooms, right through to brand-new riverside chalets. If you have the time, stay here for more than one night; it's the perfect place to take time out.

Above from far left: country lodge; Edgewater Palms Apartments and pool *(see p.114).*

Price guide for a double room with bathroom for one night:	
$$$$$	over NZ$350
$$$$	NZ$250–350
$$$	NZ$150–250
$$	NZ$100–150
$	below NZ$100

You can generally expect a good standard of dining in New Zealand. Chefs have high-quality local ingredients to work with, including fresh fruits and vegetables and an enviable range of freshwater and saltwater fish, game and farmed meat. Servings are often hearty, and in many places a main course may be enough. The list below is not intended to be comprehensive, but instead features our top choices, especially for evening dining, across the country.

Auckland

Cibo

91 St Georges Bay Road, Parnell; tel: 09 303 9660; www.cibo.co.nz; $$$

Tucked away in an old chocolate factory, Cibo does Mediterranean plus Asian-influenced cuisine. The well-executed dishes and superb service have kept it at the top for over a decade.

Dine by Peter Gordon

Skycity, 90 Federal Street; tel: 09 363 7030; www.skycitygrand.co.nz; $$$

Excellent service and an exciting menu of fusion food created by one of New Zealand's top chefs. Reservations are essential.

Price guide for a two-course meal for one with a glass of house wine:

$$$$	above NZ$80
$$$	NZ$60–80
$$	NZ$40–60
$	below NZ$40

Harbourside Seafood Bar and Grill

1st floor, Ferry Building, 99 Quay Street; tel: 09 307 0556; www.harboursiderestaurant.co.nz; $$$

Fine dining on the waterfront with wonderful views of the harbour. The seafood is super-fresh and delicious; try a Seafood Platter to share, an incredible dish featuring sashimi, sushi, prawn mayonnaise, smoked salmon, scampi, grilled fish scallops, steamed mussels, Thai fish cakes, pipi, cockles, garlic prawns and chilli squid!

Observatory Restaurant

Level 52, Sky Tower; tel: 09 363 6000; www.skycityauckland.co.nz; $$$

Venture nearly 200m (660ft) up Auckland's tallest structure to the highest restaurant in the tower for buffet-style New Zealand fare including a range of meats, seafood and vegetarian choices. Note that admission to the Sky Tower's main observation deck and the Sky Lounge Café and Bar are complimentary for Observatory guests 45 minutes prior to dining. To get the most out of the experience aim to be seated at least 30 minutes before the sun sets.

Wildfire

Shed 22, Princes Wharf; tel: 09 353 7595; www.wildfirerestaurant.co.nz; $$–$$$

Wildfire specialises in Churrasco Brazilian-style barbecue fare, in which long skewers of New Zealand beef, chicken, pork, Wildfire sausages, lamb, ribs and fish are basted with traditional marinades, and gently roasted over a pit

of glowing coals. Waiters serve sizzling-hot slices of roasted meats directly to your table until you can eat no more.

Northland

Gannets Restaurant

York Street, Russell; tel: 09 403 7990; www.gannets.co.nz; $$

Popular with the local crowd, Gannets offers a varied menu with lots of seafood and good vegetarian options. Aside from its fresh seafood, its lemongrass and ginger *crème brûlée* is marvellous, however flavours do change daily.

Kamakura

The Strand, Russell; tel: 09 403 7771; www.kamakura.co.nz; $$–$$$

It's hard to resist Kamakura's water-front location. It's the perfect setting on a balmy evening with its outdoor tables set beneath giant, sprawling pohutukawa trees right by the beach. Oysters – hand-picked from nearby Orongo Bay daily – are all the rage, but the menu is wide-ranging and there is something for everyone.

Coromandel

The Grange Road Café

7 Grange Road, Hahei; tel: 07 866 3502; $–$$

Good old-fashioned home-cooked comfort food and relaxed courtyard and deck dining.

Rotorua

Abracadabra Café/Bar

1263 Amohia Street; tel: 07 348 3883; $–$$

A Moroccan-themed café open all day with tapas and meze served from 5pm until closing. Excellent value for money.

Bistro 1284

1284 Eruera Street; tel: 07 346 1284; www.bistro1284.co.nz; $$–$$$

Attractively set in an historic 1930s building, this restaurant continually wins a range of awards and remains at the top of its game in Rotorua city for its delicious New Zealand and inter-national cuisine.

Cableway Restaurant

185 Fairy Springs Road; tel: 07 347 0027; www.skylineskyrides.co.nz; $$$

First-rate buffet with the bonus of a ride in a gondola to its hilltop site. Aim to be seated in time for sunset.

Taupo

Pimentos

17 Tamamutu Street; tel: 07 377 4549; $$–$$$

A popular evening eatery open Wed–Mon from 5.30pm. Slow-cooked lamb shanks are a speciality and the current hot favourite is infused in honey and soy.

Wellington

Arbitrageur

125 Featherston Street; tel: 04 499 5530; $$$

This is the place to see – and be seen – in Wellington. Exquisite food served in an elegant 1930s European ambience. Enormous wine list featuring some 600-odd bottles, 60 of which are available by the glass.

Above from far left: finishing touches; bowl of mussels; vines; delicious New Zealand lamb.

New Zealand Specialities
New Zealand's 'Pacific Rim' cuisine style takes its inspiration from regions and countries such as Europe, Thailand, Malaysia, Indonesia, Polynesia, Japan and Vietnam. For dishes with a distinctly New Zealand flavour, look out for dishes made with lamb, venison, salmon, crayfish, Bluff oysters, *paua* (abalone), mussels, scallops, kumara, kiwi fruit or tamarillo. Be sure to sample New Zealand's national dessert, pavlova, made from meringue, topped with lashings of fresh whipped cream and seasonal fresh fruit.

Local Wine
New Zealand's long
growing season and
cool maritime or
sub-alpine climate
provides ideal
conditions for
producing wine.
New Zealand's
major grape-
growing areas
include the sunny
eastern regions of
Gisborne and
Hawke's Bay,
Marlborough in the
northeast of the
South Island, and
the sub-alpine
valleys of Queens-
town and Central
Otago. Vineyards
are also found in
Northland, Auck-
land, Martin-
borough, Nelson
and Canterbury.

Boulcott Street Bistro

99 Boulcott Street; tel: 04 499
4199; www.boulcottstreet
bistro.co.nz; $$$

This fine restaurant, housed in a pretty
cottage just off Willis Street, has an air
of relaxed formality and serves a range
of fine fare, all stylishly presented.

Logan Brown Restaurant & Bar

192 Cuba Street; tel: 04 801 5114;
www.loganbrown.co.nz; $$$$

One of the city's top restaurants, beau-
tifully set in a 1920s bank, this place
does contemporary classics using top-
quality New Zealand produce. Book
well in advance to secure a table.

Shed 5 Restaurant & Bar

Shed 5, Queens Wharf; tel: 04 499
9069; www.shed5.co.nz; $$$

Smart seafood (and meat dishes) by
the water in a spacious, renovated
1880s wool shed.

The Tasting Room

2 Courtenay Place; tel: 04 384
1159; www.thetastingroom.co.nz; $

Located in the heart of the entertainment district, this casual gastropub
offers a range of 'tasting plates' to
accompany its wide range of beers.

The Wairarapa

Wendy Campbell's French Bistro

3 Kitchener Street, Martinborough;
tel: 06 306 8863; $$$

A small restaurant specialising in
regional produce teamed with the

local wines for which this area is
renowned. The handwritten menu is
always well thought out. Open from
6.15pm daily.

Picton/Blenheim

Twelve Trees Restaurant

Allan Scott Wines and Estate,
Jacksons Road; tel: 03 572 7123;
www.allanscott.com; $$

The menu here showcases Allan Scott's
full-bodied wines. Gorgeous indoor/
outdoor setting fewer than ten minutes
out of town on the way to the airport.

Dunedin and Otago

Bennu Restaurant

12 Moray Place; tel: 03 474 5055; $$

An upmarket brassiere serving imag-
inative Pacific Rim flavours, delicious
Mediterranean style gourmet pizzas,
and a selection of desserts, served
amid the stylish decor of the old
Savoy building.

Etrusco at the Savoy

8A Moray Place, Dunedin; tel: 03 477
3737; www.etrusco.co.nz; $$–$$$

Located on the first floor of the his-
toric Savoy Building, Etrusco offers an
extensive menu of Tuscan favourites
including a range of pasta dishes and
thin-crust pizzas, Italian breads and
antipasti, and an extensive wine list.
For after, there's strong Italian coffee,
and a delicious range of desserts
including tiramisu and pecan pie.

The Palms Restaurant

18 Queens Gardens; tel: 03 477
6534; $$

A favourite amongst the locals, this elegant, relaxed restaurant serves up generous portions from a varied menu. Enjoy lovely views over the Queens Gardens (on summer evenings) from the huge windows of this spacious turn-of-the-century building.

Franz Josef Glacier

Blue Ice

SH6, Franz Josef Village; tel: 03 752 0707; $$

Popular with locals and visitors alike, this great café/restaurant offers an à la carte menu of Pacific Rim and classic New Zealand dishes plus staples such as pizza.

The Landing

SH6, Franz Josef Village; tel: 03 752 0229; $

For good service, large portions and reasonable prices head to this laid-back café on Franz Josef's main thoroughfare. There are cosy couches inside as well as a large outdoor dining area. People come from far and wide for The Landing's hearty roast-pork dinners.

Queenstown

The Bathhouse

15–28 Marine Parade; tel: 03 442 5625; www.bathhouse.co.nz; $$$–$$$$

Located in an authentic Victorian bathhouse with scenic views of the waterfront. The romantic old-world ambience belies the innovative fusion cuisine served.

The Birches

146 Arthur's Point Road; tel: 03 441 0288; www.distinctionqueenstown. co.nz; $$$$

Located at the luxury Nugget Point Resort, ten minutes away from downtown Queenstown, this restaurant is well worth the detour to sample a range of creative and innovative Pacific-inspired dishes.

The Bunker

Cow Lane; tel: 03 441 8030; www.thebunker.co.nz; $$$–$$$$

This small, stylish restaurant serves simple, fresh, modern cuisine. Reservations are essential.

Lone Star

14 Brecon Street; tel: 03 442 9995; $$

As the name implies, this is a cowboy-themed restaurant, serving North American classics such as burgers, ribs and Dixie chicken. Huge portions.

Minami Jujisei

45 Beach Street; tel: 03 442 9854; $$

Award-winning Japanese restaurant that does traditional dishes with a modern twist. Menu includes sushi, sashimi, tempura, soups and set meals.

Price guide for a two-course meal for one with a glass of house wine:

$$$$	above NZ$80
$$$	NZ$60–80
$$	NZ$40–60
$	below NZ$40

Regional Cuisine
Every region of New Zealand has its own gourmet delights. Northland has award-winning cheeses and subtropical fruit. Rotorua is the place for a *hangi* – a traditional Maori feast cooked in an underground oven. Marlborough offers scallops and green lipped mussels; Canterbury the best racks of lamb; and in Bluff, a foodie's world revolves around the biggest, fattest oysters imaginable.

No Smoking
To protect from the adverse health effects of passive smoking, lighting up in bars, cafés and restaurants is prohibited in New Zealand.

CREDITS

Insight Step by Step New Zealand
Written by: Craig Dowling and Donna Blaber
Updated by: Donna Blaber
Series Editor: Sarah Sweeney
Cartography Editors: Zoë Goodwin and James Macdonald
Picture Manager: Steven Lawrence
Art Editor: Ian Spick

Photography by: Apa/Andy Belcher 2B, 2M, 2ML, 2MR,2TL, 2TR, 3BL, 3BR, 3ML, 3MR, 4B, 4M, 4T, 5B, 5M, 5T, 6, 9, 11, 12, 16B, 16M, 16MT, 24MM, 26, 26B, 27, 28, 28B, 29, 30, 33, 34, 38TR, 39, 40, 41, 41B, 41M, 42B, 42TL, 44, 44TL, 47, 49, 50, 52, 55, 56B, 57, 58, 58TL, 61, 62–3, 65, 67, 68, 71BR, 76–7, 76T, 78–9, 79, 80, 82, 85, 86, 87, 87B, 87M, 88–9, 88, 88B, 88TL, 89B, 90–1, 90TL, 91, 91TR, 92, 92TL, 92TR, 93TR, 94TL, 94TR, 95, 96, 98, 98T, 101, 103, 104, 116TM; Bay of Plenty Tourism 47TR, 102; Donna Blaber 11B, 14TR, 15B, 15TL,18B, 55, 65, 65B, 65M, 66TL, 77T, 78TL, 79TR, 85TL, 79TR, 85TL, 85TR; Canterbury Tourism 8L, 84TR, 106; Tourism Dunedin 71T, 72TL, 72TR, 73TL, 73TR, 74, 75; Destination Rotorua 22b, 49TR, 52–3; Maarten Holl 21B; Hans Hubler 63TR; Heritage Hotels 61T; iStockPhoto 2BL, 2BR, 4 2nd from top, 8–9, 8BM, 8MR, 10B, 12TL, 14B, 14M, 17B, 18–19, 18M, 18TL, 19TR, 24BL, 24BM, 24ML, 28T, 30TL, 31TR, 32, 34-35, 34TL, 42TR, 43TL, 43TR, 44–5, 45TR, 46B, 46TL, 48TL, 53M, 54B, 54T, 58–9, 67TR, 78B, 81TR, 89TR, 95TL, 100–1; Kelly Tarlton's Antarctic Adventure 33B; Kiwi Encounter 80TL; Mary Evans 22T, 23T; NZ Tourism 13TR, 20T; 36–7, 36B, 36M, 37TR, 38TL, 39TL, 39TR, 40TL, 41TR; NZ Tourism/Adventure Films 6BL, 33B, 109; NZ Tourism/Julian Apse 24T, 28–9; NZ Tourism/Rob Brown 12B; NZ Tourism/ Chris Cameron 25T; NZ Tourism/Ben Crawford 4 3rd from top, 24MR, 46–7, 52TL, 95TR, 97, 100BM, 103, 110; NZ Tourism/Gareth Eyres 35, 40–1, 57T, 86–7, 100MR, 104, 105; NZ Tourism/Arno Gasteiger 59; NZ Tourism/ James Heremaia 8ML, 53b, 82B; NZ Tourism/ Legend Photography 12MT, 50TL; NZ Tourism/Fay Looney 10TL, 83T; NZ Tourism, Chris McLennan 2–3, 6T, 7MR, 12TR, 16–17, 50–1, 51TR, 53TR; NZ Tourism/Hiroshi Nameeda 2BM, 12MB, 24BR, 66B, 70T, 96–7; NZ Tourism/Nick Servian 2M, 33M; NZ Tourism/Gilbert van Reenan 11TL, 11TR; NZ Tourism/Kieran Scott 33T, 36TL, 62M, 64T, 74TL, 75TL, 100MM, 120TR, 121TL, 123; NZ Tourism/Mark Smith; NZ Tourism/Rob Suisted 4 4th from top, 7BR, 7T, 24–5, 27, 56T, 68TL; NZ Tourism/Ian Trafford 4 5th from top, 6BR, 7BL, 10TR, 60T, 69T, 108; NZ Tourism/Scott Venning 33MT; NZ Tourism/David Wall 4T, 8M, 44B, 58B; NZ Tourism/Zorb Rotorua 107; Positively Welington 4B, 6MR, 7ML, 61T; Rex Features 82T, 84; Sky Tower 48–9; Southland Tourism 6L, 10M; Te Papa Museum 62TL; Treble Cone Ski 87T; Waitakere Estate 112T; Emily Walker 21T; Zorb Rororua 107.

Front cover: main image: 4Corners Images; bottom left and right: iStockphoto.
Back cover: bottom left and right: iStockphoto
Printed by: CTPS-China

Second Edition 2010
Reprinted 2011

www.insightguides.com

DISTRIBUTION

Worldwide
APA Publications GmbH & Co. Verlag KG
(Singapore branch)
7030 Ang Mo Kio Ave 5
08-65 Northstar @ AMK, Singapore 569880
Email: apasin@singnet.com.sg

UK and Ireland
GeoCenter International Ltd
Meridian House, Churchill Way West
Basingstoke, Hampshire RG21 6YR
Email: sales@geocenter.co.uk

US
Ingram Publisher Services
One Ingram Blvd, PO Box 3006
La Vergne, TN 37086-1986
Email: customer.service@ingrampublisher
services.com

Australia
Universal Publishers
PO Box 307
St. Leonards NSW 1590
Email: sales@universalpublishers.com.au

CONTACTING THE EDITORS

We would appreciate it if readers would alert us
to errors or outdated information by writing to
us at insight@apaguide.co.uk or APA Publications,
PO Box 7910, London SE1 1WE, UK.

INDEX

A

accommodation **112–9**
Achilles Point **34**
airports **109**
Akaroa **76–9**
  Harbour **79**
  Langlois-Eteveneaux
    Cottage **78**
  Museum **77**
  Old French Cemetery **78**
  St Patrick's Church **78**
All Blacks **29**
America's Cup **23, 26, 27**
Ancient Kauri Kingdom **40**
ANZAC **22**
Aoraki Mount Cook **84–5**
aquariums **33, 50, 69**
Army Memorial Museum **59**
Arrowtown **95–7**
  Chinese Camp **97**
  Dorothy Browns Cinema
    96

  Lakes District Museum **96**
art galleries **32, 61, 73–4**
Arthur's Pass **86–7**
Auckland **26–32**
  Albert Park **32**
  Art Gallery (Toi o Tamaki) **32**
  Aotea Square **29**
  Auckland Domain **29**
  Civic Theatre **28**
  Ferry Building **28, 33**
  Harbour Bridge **26**
  High Court **31**
  Holy Trinity Cathedral **30**
  Maritime Museum **28**
  Old Government House **31**
  Parnell **30**
  St Mary's Church **30**
  Sky Tower **32**
  SKYCITY **28–9, 32**
  University **31–2**
  Viaduct Harbour **27–8**
  Victoria Park Market **18**
War Memorial Museum **29**
Awanui **40**

B

banking hours **106**
Barry's Bay **77**
Bay of Islands **36–9**
Baylys Beach **41**
bicycle hire **102**
birdwatching **10, 42, 90, 91, 93**
Blenheim **69, 70**
Blue and Green Lakes **52–3**
bungy-jumping **12, 24, 32, 57,
  82, 97**
buses **110**
Bushman's Museum **90**
business hours **102**

C

Cape Palliser Lighthouse **67**
Cape Reinga **39, 40**
Captain Cook **22, 37, 38, 72, 73**
car hire **111**
Cathedral Cove **44–5**
Cave Stream Scenic Reserve **86**
cheese-making **79**
Christchurch **12**
climate and seasons **12**
Coromandel Peninsula **42–5**
  Coromandel Town **44**
  Driving Creek Railway **44**
  Forest Park **43**
Coronet Peak **95**
crime and safety **102–3**
currency **106**
customs **103**

D

Devonport **34–5**
diving **45**
dolphin watching **12–13, 37,
  45, 70, 79**
drink/driving limits **65**
driving **110–11**
driving age restrictions **102**
drugs **102, 103**
Dunedin **71–3**
duty free **103**

E

electricity **103**
embassies and consulates **103–4**
emergencies **104**
entertainment **20–1**

F

Fairlie **83–4**
Featherston **65**
  Fell Engine Museum **65**
  POW Memorial **65–6**
ferries **110**
Fiordland National Park **98–9**
fishing **12, 38, 41, 44, 45, 49,
  57, 58, 78, 82**
flights **83, 85, 91, 104–5, 109**
food and drink **14–17, 120–3**
Fox Glacier **91**
Franz Josef Village and Glacier **90–1**

G

gay and lesbian travellers **104**
Geraldine **83**
geysers **52, 55**
Gibbston Valley **97**
glow-worms **89**
gold rush **22, 42–4, 88–9, 95–7**
golf **45, 69, 96**
government **13**
Green and Blue Lakes **52–3**
Greymouth **89**
  Jade Boulder Gallery **89**
  Monteith's Brewery **89**
Greytown **66**
  Cobblestones Museum **66**
gum-digging **41**

H

Hahei 44–5
Hanmer Springs 80–2
    Thermal Resort & Spa
    82
    Thrillseekers' Canyon 82
Harrison Cove's Underwater
    Observatory 99
Haruru Falls 38
health care 105
Hillary, Sir Edmund 18, 23,
    85
Hilltop 77
history 22–3
Hokianga Harbour 41
Hokitika 89
    West Coast Historical
    Museum 89
    Wild Foods Festival
    16
Hole in the Rock 37, 38
Holy Trinity Cathedral
    30
horse riding 95
Hot Water Beach 45
hotels 112–9
Huka Falls 56
Huka Prawn Farm 56
Hundertwasser, Friedensreich
    36–7

I

ice-skating 84
insect bites 105

K

Kai Iwi Lakes 41
Kaikoura 70
Kaituna River 46
kayaking 38, 44, 56
Kelly Tarlton's Underwater
    World 33
Kerikeri 39–40
    Kemp House 39
kiwi fruit 46

L

Ladies Bay 34
Lake Ellesmere 77
Lake Ferry 67
Lake Lyndon 86
Lake Ohakuri 55
Lake Paringa 91
Lake Tarawera 53
Lake Tekapo 84
language 13
laundry 105–6
Little River 77
Lord of the Rings 10, 21,
    93

M

Macetown 97
Mackenzie Country 83–4
maori culture 11, 20, 29,
    38–9, 40, 49, 52, 53,
    60, 64, 72, 77, 81, 82,
    86, 92
Maori Arts and Crafts
    Institute 52
Mangonui 40
Mansfield, Katherine 64
maps 106
marine life 33, 37, 45, 69,
    70, 79, 99
markets 15, 29, 74
Martinborough 65–7
    Palliser Estate 67
    Te Kairanga 67
    Wine Centre 66–7
Matakohe Kauri Museum
    41
media 106
medical services 105
Milford Sound
    98–9
Mission Bay 34
money 106–7
Mount Aspiring National Park
    91
Mount Cook (Aoraki) 10, 11,
    84–5, 91

Mount Maunganui
    47–8
Mount Victoria 35
mud spa 48

N

Ngawi 67
Ninety Mile Beach 36,
    39, 40
North Head 35
Northland 36–41

O

Ohakune 59
Okahu Bay 33
Okere Falls 46–7
One Tree Hill 30
opening hours 102
Opononi 41
Otago Peninsula 73–5
Otira 88

P

Paihia 37
Paparore 40
parks and gardens 28, 30, 32,
    43, 48, 61, 62, 75, 94
Pauanui 45
pharmacies 105
Picton 68–9
    Ecoworld 69
    Edwin Fox Maritime
    Museum 69
    Pink and White Terraces
    53
police 107
population 107
post offices 107
public holidays 105
Pukekura 90
Putangirua Pinnacles 67

Q

Queenstown 85, 91, 92–4, 97

Caddyshack City **93**
Gardens **94**
Kiwi Birdlife Park **93**
Lord of the Rings Tours **93**
Skyline Gondola **92–3**
Steamer Wharf Village **93**
Walter Peak **94**

R

rafting **13, 47, 58, 82,
94**
rainforest **88**
Rangitoto Island **30, 33, 35**
Rawene **41**
    Clendon House **41**
religion **107**
Remarkables mountain range
    96, 98–9
restaurants **120–3**
Ross **89–90**
Rotorua **49–52**
    Agrodome **49**
    gondola **49**
    Kuirau Park **49**
    Lake **50–1**
    Museum **51**
    Ohinemutu **50–1**
    Rainbow Farm/Springs **50**
rugby **22, 29**
Russell **37–8**
    Museum **38**
    Pompallier House **38**
Rutherford, Sir Ernest **22, 74**

S

St Heliers **34**
St Mary's Church, Auckland
    30
sand tobogganing **40, 41**
Shantytown **87, 88**
shopping **15, 18–19, 28, 30, 62,
66, 75, 83, 93, 96**
Shotover River **94, 95**
skiing **13, 58, 59, 83, 85, 86,
95**
Sky Tower **32**

skydiving **12**
smoking **107**
spas **48, 53, 57, 82**
surfing **45**

T

Tairua **45**
Tamaki Maori Village **53**
Tangiwai **59**
Tauranga District **46–8**
Taupo **54–9**
    Hot Springs **57**
Te Kanawa, Dame Kiri **18**
Te Puke **47**
Te Whanganui A Hei Marine
    Reserve **44**
telephones **107–8**
Thames **43–4**
    Goldmine Experience **43–4**
theatre **20, 28, 64, 73, 74**
thermal spas **48, 53, 57, 82**
time zones **108**
tipping **108**
toilets **108**
Tongariro National Park **58**
tourist information **108**
trains **110**
transport **10–11, 109–11**
Treaty of Waitangi **22, 36, 37,
38–9**
Turangi **58**

V

vaccinations **111**
vineyards **16–17, 66–7, 69,
70, 80, 97**
visas **103**

W

Waiheke Island **35**
Waikari **80–1**
Waimangu Volcanic Valley
    54–5
Wai-o-Tapu **55**
Waiouru **59**

Waipara Valley **80**
Waipoua Forest **41**
Wairarapa **65–7**
Waitangi National Reserve **38**
Waitemata Harbour **26, 33,
35**
Waiwera Thermal Resort **41**
Walter Peak **94**
War Memorial Museum **29**
waterfalls **36, 38, 47, 48, 53,
56, 87, 91**
Wellington **60–4**
    Beehive **62–3**
    Botanic Garden **62**
    Cable Car **62**
    City Gallery **61**
    Civic Square **61**
    Courtenay Place **64**
    Frank Kitts Park **61**
    Lambton Quay **62**
    Museum of New Zealand
        (Te Papa Tongarewa)
        60–1
    Museum of Wellington
        City and Sea **63–4**
    National Archives **63**
    Old Government Buildings
        63
    Oriental Parade **64**
Whakarewarewa **51–2**
whale-watching **12–13, 70**
whaling **70**
Whangamata **51–2**
Whangarei Falls **36**
Whataroa **90**
Whitianga **44**
White Island **48**
wineries **16–17, 66–7, 69, 70,
80, 97**
women's rights **23**

Y

yachting **23, 26, 27, 38, 49**

Z

Zorbing **49**

Tours

North Island

1	Auckland	p26
2	Around Auckland	p33
3	Northland	p36
4	Coromandel Peninsula	p42
5	Tauranga District	p46
6	Rotorua	p49
7	Taupo	p54
8	Wellington	p60
9	The Wairarapa	p65

South Island

10	Ferry to the South Island	p68
11	Dunedin and the Otago Peninsula	p71
12	Akaroa	p76
13	Hanmer Springs	p80
14	Christchurch to Queenstown	p83
15	Arthur's Pass and West Coast	p86
16	Queenstown	p92
17	Arrowtown	p95
18	Milford Sound	p98